CULTURAL CONSIDERATIONS IN ASIAN AND PACIFIC ISLANDER AMERICAN MENTAL HEALTH

To Dr R Needlam

Kenneth Guy

Cultural Considerations in Asian and Pacific Islander American Mental Health

EDITED BY Harvette Grey
AND Brittany N. Hall-Clark

OXFORD
UNIVERSITY PRESS

OXFORD
UNIVERSITY PRESS

Oxford University Press is a department of the University of
Oxford. It furthers the University's objective of excellence in research,
scholarship, and education by publishing worldwide.

Oxford   New York
Auckland   Cape Town   Dar es Salaam   Hong Kong   Karachi
Kuala Lumpur   Madrid   Melbourne   Mexico City   Nairobi
New Delhi   Shanghai   Taipei   Toronto

With offices in
Argentina   Austria   Brazil   Chile   Czech Republic   France   Greece
Guatemala   Hungary   Italy   Japan   Poland   Portugal   Singapore
South Korea   Switzerland   Thailand   Turkey   Ukraine   Vietnam

Oxford is a registered trademark of Oxford University Press
in the UK and certain other countries.

Published in the United States of America by
Oxford University Press
198 Madison Avenue, New York, NY 10016

© Oxford University Press 2015

Library of Congress Cataloging-in-Publication Data
Cultural considerations in Asian and Pacific Islander American mental health / edited by
Harvette Grey, Brittany N. Hall-Clark.
   p. ; cm.
Includes bibliographical references and index.
ISBN 978-0-19-024337-1 (pb : alk. paper)
I. Grey, Harvette, editor.   II. Hall-Clark, Brittany N., editor.
[DNLM: 1. Asian Americans—ethnology—United States.   2. Mental
Health—ethnology—United States.   3. Mental Disorders—ethnology—United
States.   4. Mental Disorders—therapy—United States.   5. Oceanic Ancestry
Group—ethnology—United States.   6. Socioeconomic Factors—United States.
WA 305 AA1]
RC451.5.A75
616.890089′95073—dc23
2015000070

9 8 7 6 5 4 3 2 1
Printed in the United States of America
on acid-free paper

Contents

Foreword

This writer was in attendance at a local city council meeting years ago, together with other service providers and representatives of community-based organizations requesting funds for vital employment, social, child care, and other services. Representatives would take turns standing up and speaking on behalf of the organizations they represented. One such representative of a community-based organization that served Blacks stood up and spoke. As he was making his points to city council and to the crowd of people in attendance, he turned and gestured to me; he had a serious and determined look on his face, hoping to drive home a point with this writer's acknowledgment, and declared, "Tony, you speak Asian, and you know what I mean, right?"

The term *Asian* or *Asians* evolved from an antiquated, offensive, and derogatory term originally used to describe the ethnicities and cultures of this group, namely, *Oriental.* Just as Blacks fought to eventually erase the term *Negro* from this nation's political and cultural collective consciousness, the battle to eliminate use of the term *Oriental* was won, and the term was replaced by the word *Asian.* The word *Oriental* objectified Asians and is now considered politically incorrect. Now this term is used ironically to describe objects as opposed to people, such as *Oriental art* or *Oriental rug.* (Refer to "'Ornamental Orientals' and Others: Ethnic Labels in Review,'" Benjamin Tong, *Focus*, 4, 2, June 1990). The word *Asian* is casually used to describe a group whose facial features appear similar but who are, in fact, of different nationalities, cultures, and ancestries.

The term *Asian* also is an Asian American phenomenon. Foreign-born people from Asia do not describe themselves as Asians. Rather, they describe themselves as a specific ethnicity from the country of their birth and upbringing. In "'Ornamental Orientals,'" Tong writes, "Asian American is of a recent coinage" and "was... initially heard at San Francisco State University during the now historic 1968–1969 Student-Faculty Strike [at which this writer was both a student and strike participant] for the creation of the very first American college program in ethnic studies."

Asian is also a politically convenient term. After President Lyndon B. Johnson's declaration of War on Poverty in 1964, a number of ethnic community-based organizations (CBOs) sprang up to meet the needs of Black, Latino, and Asian communities. His declaration enabled communities to receive government funding to help break the cycle of poverty. Many Asian groups formed to serve the specific communities they represented. *Chinese, Korean, Japanese, Vietnamese*, and other specific nationalities preceded the titles of their CBOs.

As funding became scarce, many CBOs were compelled to unite and offer services under one roof. This was what happened in the Asian community. Many groups formed, with the title *Asian* preceding the service it offered to the community to attract funding. They provided services to a group of people with different ethnicities, cultures, and languages.

Race, language, and culture are the cornerstones in working with Asians. Race, language, and culture not only define one's identity but also one's conscious and unconscious history, whether one was born in America or abroad.

America has been described metaphorically as a melting pot or as a salad bowl of peoples and cultures. The melting pot view holds that there are different types of people living together in this society who gradually create one community. The salad bowl view connotes a pluralistic society of people mixed together but continuing to maintain their different traditions, languages, and interests. In the Asian or Asian American psychological literature describing these characterizations, the former is referred to as *assimilation* and the latter as *acculturation*. (See discussion about the assimilation and acculturation of the Marginal Man in "Chinese-American Personality and Mental Health," *Amerasia, 1,* 1, 1971, by Stanley Sue and Derald Sue.)

This writer's research and dissertation topic concerned mental health issues among unemployed non-English-speaking (NES) or limited-English-speaking (LES) Asians. Although it is essential that service providers be able to speak and understand the native language of clients they are treating or counseling, consideration and awareness of the client's culture, race, and generation when treating both American-born and foreign-born Asians are also essential. In my research, I posit that mental health concerns such as depression, anxiety, self-doubt, domestic violence, and anger are manifested when people are unemployed for long periods of time. Because of cultural constraints, Asians generally will not seek mental health counseling: loss of face, guilt, and being stigmatized by their culture are examples of self-imposed barriers due to cultural upbringing or expectations. (In Chapter 1, Hwang and Ting point out that "cultural competence requires therapist cultural self-awareness as well as understanding of the client.")

When providing mental health or other services to an Asian client, the service provider should consider clients' cultural generation and the family's multigenerational structure or "multicultural identities" (Melba Vasquez, "Foreword," *Cultural Considerations in Latino American Mental Health,* Grey & Hall-Clark, 2015). Many NES and LES families live in extended-family situations in which three or more generations of family members live together. How old is the client? What country is the client from? Is the client a refugee from a war-torn country? (In their discussion of the mental health needs of elder refugees who have come to the United States in Chapter 3, Nagata, Tsai-Chae, and Nguyen write that "there are...elder refugees who came to the United States fleeing genocide and political or economic crises.") What are the clients' country's expectations of a person that age and with that position in the family? Do clients' parents play a strong role in the family structure? The treatment outcome may well depend on how well-informed and sensitive the service provider is to the client's age and position in the family in the approach to treatment.

Maslow's hierarchy of needs ("A Theory of Human Motivation," *Psychological Review, 50*, 4, July 1943) describes five levels of needs, generally depicted in a pyramid with the most basic needs, physiological and safety, forming the bottom of the pyramid. These two needs are characterized as concrete or basic needs (a person needs food, water, and shelter to meet physiological needs). Similarly, safety needs, such as security and stability, on the next level of the pyramid must be met before people progress to the next levels on the pyramid.

Unemployed people naturally have a number of basic or concrete needs due primarily to their bad pecuniary circumstances. However, the longer unemployed people cannot find a job to help satisfy their basic needs, the greater the psychological and social pressure they will feel to find a job. They begin to worry and their self-esteem begins to wane as they become depressed, angry, violent, or otherwise distressed in the process of trying to find a job to subsist. Hwang and Ting in Chapter 1 discuss how "specific psychosocial stressors" are "associated with the prevalence of depression." Thus, as people's basic needs are met, they will feel more mentally healthy.

Despite the public's greater awareness of both the need for and the efficacy of mental health services nowadays as compared with the past, both the general population and Asian populations are still reluctant to readily seek mental health services. On the other hand, these populations will readily seek specific social services to help satisfy their basic or concrete needs. Although this is also true for the unemployed NES and LES, they often cannot even begin to find help for their social service, employment, legal, child care, housing, health, or even mental health needs because of the paucity of bilingual social service and mental health counselors.

The four chapters of this book not only provide background and insight into some of the issues and concerns regarding the mental health treatment of Asians but also discuss the demographics, the history of discrimination, cultural values, linguistic aspects, and a general perspective of Asians in America. Although these insights and background are not the focus of these chapters, they do provide a contextual framework for the reader to consider in rendering mental health services to the Asian community.

Although this writer's colleague at the city council meeting assumed that all Asians speak a language called "Asian," it is hoped that the reader will appreciate and understand that the word *Asian* is merely a descriptor, much as books on a bookshelf are described as *books*. Upon examination, each book is different, has its own title, and tells its own story. Similarly, upon examination, each Asian group is different and has its own culture, heritage, customs, and language. The therapist who works with Asians must be aware of the differences in language and culture across each of the ethnic groups that fall under the generalized term *Asian*. For therapists, understanding the culture, history, and language of the ethnic group they are treating may be the key to a psychological breakthrough. But even more important, this understanding can and will establish trust between the client and the therapist.

Tony Leong Jr., PhD
Oakland, CA
June 2014

Preface

Due to my interest in culture, which was enhanced by the late Mervin Freedman, dean and cofounder of the Wright Institute, and because of my involvement in various projects relating to ethnicity, culture, and race, I was contacted by Joan Bossert, editor at Oxford University Press, and offered the opportunity to produce a book on culture and mental health treatment. After speaking with the late Asa Hilliard, a mentor and an esteemed scholar, I also spoke with the president of the American Psychological Association at the time, who also encouraged me to pursue the opportunity. I am grateful to all of the aforementioned. I am also thankful to my co-editor, Brittany Hall-Clark, whom I met when she was presenting at the Association of Black Psychologists' annual conference as a graduate student in 2009. Due to her interest in and knowledge of cultural considerations in mental health treatment, I invited her to join this project after it was underway, and she has been invaluable. Brittany Hall-Clark is now Brittany Hall-Clark, PhD, a licensed psychologist. Big thanks go to our Oxford editor, Sarah Harrington, and assistant editor, Andrea Zekus. Their support was unwavering.

For this book, I chose to recruit multicultural and racially/ethnically diverse scholars to discuss their own racial and ethnic groups in the context of the selected subjects. I felt that it was important for members of certain ethnic and racial minorities to tell their own stories in a way that was comfortable and natural.

The perspective taken within these pages is that the most important aspect of mental health treatment is the client's experience of healing and growth, which measures the successes of a particular method with that particular client. Most of the contributors to this book have played many roles within a myriad of groups—as cultural interpreters, healers, historians. Many, if not all, are in regular contact with their own and perhaps other minority groups. They are exceptionally knowledgeable about the subjects they have chosen to discuss and are experts owing to their educational backgrounds, personal experiences, and racial/ethnic group membership.

Readers will find a range of presentations displaying varied degrees of acculturation and have the opportunity to experience traditional as well as nontraditional methods of addressing mental health problems. Readers would do well also to remember to step out of their own culture, teaching, and belief systems to understand and appreciate the range of diversity of ideas, morals, mores, and expressions presented here.

With the traditional, readers will find what may seem a very different and perhaps unfamiliar experience of treatment. The traditional treatment model addresses history and historical trauma, as well as the impact of historical trauma on today's behaviors, especially dysfunctional behaviors. Historical traumas are horrific past occurrences that a group has experienced. Genocide, enslavement, and incarceration of a racial/ethnic group, as well as ethnic cleansing, are examples of historical traumas that can impact the clinical relationship and a client's relationship to the environment.

Many Americans of all cultures revel in the concept of the United States as the land of the free and the home of the brave, the melting pot or the stew that mixes various cultures. In response to these ringing endorsements, immigrants often approach the United States as a place of freedom, citing political, religious, ethnic, and other types of discrimination in their home countries, perils they are seeking to escape. Thousands come each year for liberty and self-determination and to work and live better. Depending on these immigrants' language, place of origin, and especially skin pigmentation, they are often classified as part of an ethnic or racial group that might not be recognized in their country of origin. This experience can be confusing and disheartening, to say the least. Although many might think that the racial/ethnic minorities discussed in this text are labeled as such because of their physical numbers, the term *minority* may also suggest a lack of equal status and power. This alone may well contribute to anxiety, depression, and substance abuse among members of these groups. To be or to become an underclass citizen in a "land of plenty" is devastating.

One instance of being treated as an underclass citizen happened to me. I attended graduate school in Berkeley, California. One day during my last year there, I was driving my car (a small, old Karmann Ghia, with the driver's door held together with a rope) when I was stopped and surrounded by several police officers with rifles drawn. After they forced my car up on the sidewalk, guns totally surrounded me. This was in broad daylight; to say that I was terrified is an understatement, as I was alone. I thought that this was excessive force for a broken car door. Luckily, one of my psychotherapy clients, a popular and wealthy businesswoman, was driving by in her Mercedes-Benz. She had witnessed the event and began screaming for the police to leave me alone. She stopped her car, got out, and walked toward me. I got out of my car. By this time, several store owners had come out of their stores inquiring about the commotion. All of the seven or more police officers appeared to be White, while the rest of us, including the store owners, were people of color. One of the officers stated that they were seeking a Black female who had recently robbed a bank. They listed the woman as approximately 5'8", with light skin and red hair. I am 5'4", with dark skin and dark brown hair. After looking at my driver's license and eyeballing the community support, especially my client, the businesswoman, they left. Because it was broad daylight, because of the appearance of my client and the storekeepers, this story does not have a tragic ending. The tragedy was that the incident occurred at all. I share here experiences that have happened to me in order to inform the reader that racial/ethnic minority groups run the risk of having many more negative run-ins with episodes of victimization than do those in majority groups. These incidents might not ever be brought up in the therapeutic session but nevertheless contribute to how the client might tell his story and view the therapist and himself.

These kinds of occurrences are not unusual in many communities; nevertheless, they are not often mentioned or acknowledged by a client or health provider within the context of psychological therapy unless such an event is part of the presenting problem—if, say, the client is suffering from anxiety, depression, or substance abuse as an outcome of such an incident. Different groups may experience different types of harassment by various authority figures and/or members of their own community. Therefore, their view of society and self might be quite different, depending on what they view as normal.

People who live in a society that fails to protect them live their lives in the company of denial, stress, and anger, which trigger disease and unhealthy behaviors. These conditions are often the result of systemic racism that results in inequities in education, household ownership, financial savings, employment, and other areas. Hatred is a byproduct of institutional racism, as is, for many of America's minorities, self-hatred.

In reading the following pages, scholars, researchers, and clinicians might consider the following questions. How do members of ethnic and racial groups experience anxiety, depression, and/or substance abuse? Are these problems directly or indirectly related to their acculturation? Does their history impact their todays and possibly their tomorrows? Are there emotional trails that lead back to historical trauma or original injury? How can healers address the emotional trials that have affected the client but also the group? What should mental health professionals, healers, or/and cultural interpreters know about their client's culture prior to attempting to assist? The hope is that by gaining knowledge about the culture of others, these healers will be encouraged to examine their own cultures and comfort levels with members of other races/ethnicities. We must remember that culture not only identifies a person or group but also serves as the glue holding that group together. Culture is something that individuals can rely on for emotional support. Although culture can and should tell of the historical traumas of a group, it should also protect a group from being programmed for self-destruction and support the individual, family, and community. When this does not occur, one can expect dysfunctional families, as well as dysfunctional communities rampant with chronic unemployment and high crime rates. Those who provide mental health services, health care, education, and an array of other services to all ethnic groups must not only address their clients' immediate needs but also be cognizant of their culture and the role that culture plays in these clients' issues—and how it can aid in assessing problems and concerns.

Like all grad students, when I was in graduate school, I had to see clients in the school's clinic. One client was a very tall, nice-looking African American man. Upon seeing me for the first time, he said in a very loud voice, "How did I get you? Did they know I was Black when I called in? I don't know if we can work together!" He continued, "If you are a follower of Dr. Smith [a well-known African American psychiatrist], we cannot work together. I don't agree with his principles." He listed additional reasons that we could not work together. Despite this, we did work together, and these issues became less impeding as time went on. I addressed his concerns, and our rapport deepened. As we continued the process, it became more obvious that he was a victim of various forms of racism and emotional issues that contributed to his not trusting anyone—especially other Blacks and women. He initially did not trust himself or others and stated at the outset that he did not want an African American therapist; however, at some point he changed his mind and decided to give me a chance.

He continued to attend sessions for 2 years. My supervisors were instrumental in guiding me though this challenging case. One asked me if I was a plumber or a therapist. A plumber gets the stuff out, but the therapist gets it out and then repairs the toilet, pipes, and drain. The therapist makes sure that things are working properly. We hear clients' pain and anger and assist them in building trust and strength. That is our duty.

This book provides a focused account of the relationship between mental health and culture within the Asian and Pacific Islander American communities. The topics discussed are acculturation, depression, and substance abuse. These topics are not all-inclusive but what the chapter authors determined were issues of leading importance in the clinical treatment of these populations. The Asian community includes a myriad of ethnic groups and nationalities with different cultures, languages, histories, and customs. In other words, there is no one Asian language or Asian culture. Asians are often categorized as the model minority, stereotyped as being rich and well-educated; when problems such as poverty or racism arise, society assumes that Asians can take care of their own problems within their respective communities. These and other stereotypes foster the belief that Asians do not suffer poverty and racism in this society like other ethnic and racial minorities. This, of course, is far from the truth. There is much economic diversity within the Asian community, with a fair number of Southeast Asians (Vietnamese, Cambodians, and Laotians) highly dependent on welfare (*New York Times*, May 19, 1994). Unemployment and poverty among Asians in dense populations such as the San Francisco Bay area, for example, remain high according to the 2010 U.S. Bureau of the Census. Within Asian communities, several groups have significant rates of poverty, such as the Hmong (37.8%), Cambodians (29.3%), Laotians (18.5%), and Vietnamese (16.6%; New America Medici Ethno blog 2010). The same source states that for Asian seniors 65 and older, the poverty rate is 12.3%. This is higher than the national average for all seniors, which is 9.9%. White seniors are cited as having a 7.8% poverty rate. Usually poverty rates are higher in urban areas. For example, Philadelphia is listed as having a 41% poverty rate for Cambodians, 33% for Chinese, and 31% for Vietnamese (Philly.com). According to the *New York Times* website (The Local: East Village, April 25, 2011; http://eastvillage.thelocal.nytimes.com/2011/04/25/more-asian-tenants-in-public-housing/), the percentage of Asian tenants residing in public housing in New York City's East Village neighborhood rose from 11.5% in 2000 to 14.3% in 2012. Non-English- and limited-English-speaking impoverished Asians make up a high percentage of those on the welfare rolls and those who are collecting food stamps. They also make up a significant percentage of those living in low-income housing projects, underscoring the poverty rate among Asians. Not only are Asians victims of racism by the majority community but also they are victims of racism by the ethnic minority community.

This book addresses selected mental health issues pertaining to various Asian groups in America. We hope that this book will assist the reader in better understanding the importance of cultural considerations in the mental health treatment of diverse populations.

Harvette Grey, PhD
October 2014

About the Editors

Harvette Grey, PhD, is the former Executive Director of the Cultural Center and Founding Director of the Women's Center at DePaul University. She is also past President of the Association of Black Psychologists. Dr. Grey has had a wide range of professional experience, from community psychologist to an administrator in several settings. Her specialties include providing and designing culturally focused services and treatments for America's racial and ethnic minority populations.

Brittany Hall-Clark, PhD, is an Assistant Professor at the University of Texas Health Science Center at San Antonio. She works with the STRONG STAR multidisciplinary PTSD research consortium, primarily as a research therapist. She completed her PhD in clinical psychology at the University of Texas at Austin. Her research interests include culturally competent treatment, cultural variables in mental health, and racial/ethnic differences in PTSD.

Contributors

Wei-Chin Hwang, PhD, is a Professor of Psychology at Claremont McKenna College. He received his PhD from the clinical psychology program at UCLA (2003), completed his predoctoral fellowship at Richmond Area Multi-Services (RAMS)—National Asian American Psychology Training Center, and completed a clinical-research postdoctoral fellowship at Harbor UCLA Medical Center. His research focuses on understanding and reducing mental health disparities, psychotherapy process and outcomes, improving therapist cultural competency and effectiveness when working with people from different backgrounds, and developing models and frameworks for culturally adapting therapy for ethnic minorities. He is also a licensed clinical psychologist with an independent practice in Pasadena and Claremont, California.

Soni Kim, PsyD, is a licensed clinical psychologist and founder and director of Crossroads Institute for Psychotherapy and Assessment, located in Southern California. She was an adjunct Associate Professor at USC's Marriage and Family Therapy program, and currently provides consultation and supervision on child and adult psychotherapy and assessment to psychologists and trainees, with a particular emphasis on understanding psychodynamic processes in the therapist-client relationship and the therapist-supervisor/

consultant relationship. She works as an expert witness on Asian American cultural and mental health issues in legal settings, and as a cultural consultant in research settings. Program and has extensive experience supervising mental health professionals.

Donna K. Nagata, PhD, is Professor of Psychology at the University of Michigan, Ann Arbor. Her research interests include the long-term psychosocial impacts of the World War II incarceration of Japanese Americans, Asian American mental health, intergenerational relationships, family processes, and qualitative approaches to ethnocultural research.

Teresa U. Nguyen, MS, is a Postdoctoral Fellow at the Center for Women's Health and Health Disparities Research, University of Wisconsin, Madison. Her primary research interests include ethnocultural mental health, Asian American mental health, minority and immigrant psychology, cultural conceptualization and subjective experiences of emotion, Vietnamese Americans and the psychosocial consequences of the Vietnam War and refugee experiences, intergenerational relations, and family interaction processes.

Julia Ting, PhD, is currently working full-time as a clinical psychologist at the British Columbia Operational Stress Injury Clinic and adjunct professor at the University of British Columbia. She completed her doctorate in clinical psychology at the University of Utah and her predoctoral residency at Vancouver Coastal Health. Her primary research interests focus on understanding the barriers to receiving mental health care.

Amy H. Tsai-Chae, PhD, is a licensed clinical psychologist and currently works at The Children's Health Council in Palo Alto, California. She provides individual and systems-based family therapy to children and teens attending a therapeutic non-public school and also serves as a clinical supervisor to mental health interns/trainees. She completed her doctorate degree in Clinical Psychology at the University of Michigan and her postdoctoral residency at Harbor-UCLA Medical Center. Her research and practice interests include family conflict, intergenerational relationships, and Asian American mental health.

CULTURAL CONSIDERATIONS IN ASIAN AND PACIFIC ISLANDER AMERICAN MENTAL HEALTH

Treating Asian Americans: An Overview

WEI-CHIN HWANG AND JULIA TING

This book provides clinical insights on how to treat Asian Americans of various age groups, dealing with a variety of mental health problems. However, before considering the dynamics of treating Asian Americans with specific diagnoses, it is necessary to have a basic understanding of who Asian Americans are and how they are unique as a group. The term *Asian American* refers to a very diverse group of people, with different cultures, customs, languages, backgrounds, migration histories, and experiences. Although many of the Asian American groups often share similar qualities, there are cultural differences between ethnic groups.

According to the 2010 Census, Asian Americans make up 5.6% (17.3 million) of the U.S. population (Hoeffel, Rastogi, Kim, & Shahid, 2012). This number includes 14.7 million (4.8%) single-race Asian Americans and 2.6 million (0.9%) mixed-race Asian Americans. Historically, Asian Americans have suffered from discriminatory immigration laws that were reformed in 1965, with immigration to the United States surging since then. In fact, Asian Americans are proportionately the fastest growing racial group in the United States, growing 4 times faster (evidencing a 46% increase from 11.9 million in 2000 to 17.3 million in 2010) than the total U.S. population (Hoeffel et al., 2012). The majority of Asian Americans (61.9%) are foreign born (Barnes & Bennett, 2002), and the six largest groups are Chinese Americans, Filipino Americans, Asian Indian Americans, Vietnamese Americans, Korean Americans, and Japanese Americans, respectively (Hoeffel et al., 2012).

Although each of the Asian American ethnic groups is culturally unique, they share some commonalities compared with those from Western backgrounds. Lee (1997) pointed out that Eastern and Western cultural traditions place different emphases on various aspects of life. Primary among them are collectivistic versus individualistic orientation, social norms in suppression versus expression of emotions, holistic versus compartmental views on health and mental health, and differences in family roles, structure, and level of involvement.

The Need for Cultural Competence

Although mental health practitioners may move toward cultural competence when they learn about different cultures, understanding the client's culture alone is insufficient when faced with the actualities of treating someone who is culturally different from the mainstream. A common but problematic assumption made by health care professionals is that learning about the client's culture is sufficient to improve cultural competency. This overly simplistic way of thinking reinforces the problematic assumption that the difficulty of culture is located in the client as the other, rather than the cultural difference between the client and the provider.

Hardy and Laszloffy (1995) stress the importance of an interactional perspective between the client and the provider, noting that cultural competence requires therapist cultural self-awareness as well as understanding of the client. Moreover, simple ethnic matching of patient and provider may not necessarily result in more efficacious outcomes if the practitioner has not been trained to be culturally competent. Self-awareness involves understanding one's own racism (including racism toward other groups as well as internalized racism or racism toward one's own group) and the role of privilege in the therapeutic relationship and other interactions between different ethnic groups. These topics can be uncomfortable to talk about and work through but are essential in the development of cultural competency for clinicians.

The most widely accepted definition of *cultural competency* refers to the possession of cultural self-awareness, knowledge, and skills that facilitate delivery of effective services to ethnically and culturally diverse clientele (Sue, 1982; Sue, Arredondo, & McDavis, 1992; Sue, Zane, Hall, & Berger, 2009). In describing the complexities of cultural competence, Lo and Fung (2003) add that it is also important to distinguish between generic and specific cultural competencies, that is, the knowledge and skill set needed in any cross-cultural encounter as opposed to that which is necessary to work with a specific ethnocultural group.

Approaching the treatment of Asian Americans requires the clinician to be dynamic and cognitively flexible because of pervasive stereotypes that plague Asian Americans and that are reinforced by media images (Sue, 1998). In talking about her experiences working with her previous White therapist, an Asian American client told one of the authors that there were times when she really enjoyed working with the White therapist but also times when she felt uncomfortable because she felt the therapist would make culturally insensitive comments or stereotype her in her attempts to be empathic (e.g., by saying that it seems like finances and real estate are really important for all Asians). Even when practitioners try to learn about treating Asian Americans in good faith, the manner in which trainings and readings are structured and the strong tendency for readers to take away only a few major points can sometimes result in the negative effect of reinforcing stereotypes and producing even more rigid viewpoints. Practitioners need to be aware of such dynamics if they are to develop their skills in treating Asian American clients.

Challenges in Treating Asian Americans

Clinical experience tells us that psychotherapy can be beneficial for Asian Americans, if conducted in a culturally competent and sensitive manner. However, there has been very little research verifying the treatment efficacy of psychotherapy for Asian Americans. More empirical evidence documenting how Asian Americans respond to psychotherapeutic treatment and determining what factors influence treatment progress is needed. The limited empirical evidence indicates that Asian American clients are less likely to seek formal mental health services (Hu, Snowden, Jerrell, & Nguyen, 1991; Snowden & Cheung, 1990), likely to be severely ill at point of entry (Lin & Lin, 1978; Meyer, Zane, Cho, & Takeuchi, 2009; Sue, 1977; Sue & Sue, 1987), and more likely to have worse treatment outcomes or drop out of treatment prematurely than other groups (Sue, 1977; Zane, Enomoto, & Chun, 1994). There is also some evidence to indicate that Asian Americans born in the United States are more likely to seek mental health treatment than those who are foreign born (Meyer et al., 2009). Taken together, these findings suggest that practitioners need to be wary when treating Asian Americans, who may be at a particularly high risk for treatment failure and who may be ambivalent about seeking help.

Practitioners face a number of additional dilemmas that complicate the treatment process for Asian Americans. For example, linguistic barriers and lack of linguistic competence reduce our ability to treat immigrant Asians. Moreover, many Asian Americans have had little exposure to mental health education and may strongly adhere to cultural stereotypes that those who are mentally ill are "crazy." Individual, family, and community stigma toward mental illness can have a detrimental impact on whether clients seek help and affect how they are perceived by others (Corrigan, 2004). Cultural differences in communicating mental distress can contribute to mental health care underutilization (e.g., whether and where they seek help). For example, some scholars report that Asians and Asian

Americans are more likely than European Americans to express their distress somatically and are also more likely to seek help from a primary care physician than from a mental health provider (Chun, Enomoto, & Sue, 1996). However, this does not mean that all Asian Americans somatize because many do express their psychological symptoms and emotions while in treatment, especially after a therapeutic alliance is developed (Cheung, 1985; Cheung & Lau, 1982). Practitioners need to be careful not to stereotype patients based on their cultural backgrounds and should remain flexible in exploring various hypotheses.

When working with Asian Americans, practitioners need to be aware that they are a group in transition (Lee, 1997). Asian Americans come to the United States at different life stages, with different immigration experiences (e.g., voluntary or involuntary), and with different degrees of exposure to Western culture, and they acculturate at different speeds, depending on where they are coming from, where they relocate, their age of immigration, and their level of education. As a result, the problems that they face and the stresses that they experience may vary widely and may be influenced by acculturative processes, including struggles with forming an ethnic identity and culturally influenced family conflict.

Given the strong cultural emphasis on family relations, Hwang (2006a) notes that practitioners need to be particularly wary of acculturative family distancing (AFD), defined as the problematic distancing that occurs between immigrant parents and children that is a consequence of differences in acculturative processes and cultural changes that become more salient over time. Acculturative family distancing has two dimensions, a breakdown in communication and incongruent cultural values that develop as a consequence of different rates of acculturation and the resulting formation of an acculturation gap between parents and their children. These two dimensions of AFD are hypothesized to act as proximal mechanisms of the more distal construct of the acculturation gap and directly increase risk for individual and family dysfunction. Among Asian

American and Latino college students, AFD was found to be associated with increased psychological distress and greater risk for clinical depression (Hwang & Wood, 2009). Family conflict mediated the relationship between AFD and psychological outcomes. Moreover, in Chinese American families, AFD has been found to be associated with higher depressive symptoms and risk for clinical depression among high school students and their mothers (Hwang, Wood, & Fujimoto, 2010). Family conflict partially mediated this relation for youths, whereas for mothers, AFD directly increased risk for depression. This relationship held even after controlling for the general notion of the acculturation gap.

The Need for Evidence-Based Community Interventions

In recent years, there has been an initiative to establish, define, and validate empirically supported treatments (ESTs) in the United States (APA Task Force on Psychological Intervention Guidelines, 1995; Task Force on Promotion and Dissemination of Psychological Procedures, 1995). Although considerable progress has been made in establishing and defining efficacious and possibly efficacious treatments for the general population, relatively little is known about the efficacy of ESTs for people from diverse ethnic and cultural backgrounds. Recent reviews underscore the limitations of EST literature, stating that few studies have been conducted confirming whether ESTs are efficacious in treating ethnic minorities, and provide several recommendations for moving beyond this impasse (Miranda et al., 2005; Nagayama-Hall, 2001).

Although we have begun to build a wealth of clinical knowledge that will help us improve the treatment of Asian Americans, a bridge between science and clinical practice needs to be built if we are to move forward. Given the differences between Eastern and Western cultures and the additional complexities associated with treating cultures in transition, we need to improve our understanding of how to best approach these challenges. For example, should we (a) implement an "as is approach" to disseminating ESTs to culturally diverse ethnic groups, (b) adapt ESTs to be more culturally congruent to better fit the needs of ethnic clients, or (c) develop new, culture-specific ESTs for Asian Americans? Implementing an "as is approach" in disseminating ESTs to ethnic minority clients may not fully address cultural differences salient to ethnic minority groups. Developing novel ethnic-specific treatments for each culturally different group in the United States may be prohibitively costly and time-consuming and lead to clinician training difficulties, especially if they are based on different theoretical paradigms.

For immigrant Asian Americans, where cultural differences are likely to be distinct and impact treatment, adapting ESTs to better address their needs may be a better and more cost-effective approach. However, the question of how to adapt therapy poses another set of challenges. Hwang (2006b) developed the psychotherapy adaptation and modification framework (PAMF) to facilitate this process. The PAMF is a theoretically driven, top-down approach that utilizes three levels of adaptation, including 6 therapeutic domains, 25 therapeutic principles, and corresponding rationales. The domains are (a) dynamic issues and cultural complexities; (b) orienting clients to psychotherapy and increasing mental health awareness; (c) understanding cultural beliefs about mental illness, its causes, and what constitutes appropriate treatment; (d) improving the client–therapist relationship; (e) understanding cultural differences in the expression and communication of distress; and (f) addressing cultural issues specific to the population. Principles and rationales can be modified according to the population for which one is adapting treatments.

Ideally, a combination of top-down and bottom-up approaches would best inform clinical science and help meet the needs of ethnic minority populations. A more comprehensive framework, the formative method for adapting psychotherapy (FMAP), is also available (Hwang, 2009). The FMAP uses a consumer community-based and iterative approach to culture and psychotherapy. The five FMAP phases target developing, testing, and reformulating therapy modifications: (a) generating knowledge and collaborating with stakeholders, (b) integrating generated information with theory and empirical and clinical knowledge, (c) reviewing the initial culturally adapted clinical intervention with stakeholders and revising the culturally adapted intervention, (d) testing the culturally adapted intervention, and (e) finalizing the culturally adapted intervention.

Although we have made some advances and better understand how to modify treatments for Asian American populations, much more work needs to be done. For example, empirical research is needed to understand naturalistic treatment outcomes, and randomized controlled trials (RCTs) are needed to test whether evidence-based treatments, as well as culturally adapted treatments, are effective in treating Asian Americans. Moreover, more clinically informative papers that use case studies to illustrate adaptations and effective techniques would benefit trainees and practitioners who strive to provide the best treatment possible. The following chapters provide readers with an introductory exposure on how to treat Asian Americans for a variety of mental health problems. However, it is important to remember that this is not an end-all and that becoming culturally competent requires continuing time, training, and effort.

References

American Psychological Association, Task Force on Psychological Intervention Guidelines. (1995). *Template for developing guidelines: Interventions for mental disorders and psychological aspects of physical disorders.* Washington, DC: Author.

Barnes, J. S., & Bennett, C. E. (2002). *The Asian population: 2000.* Current Population Reports C2KBR/01-16. Washington, DC: U.S. Census Bureau.

Cheung, F. M. (1985). An overview of psychopathology in Hong Kong with special reference to somatic presentation. In W. S. Tseng & D. Wu (Eds.), *Chinese culture and mental health* (pp. 287–300). Orlando, FL: Academic Press.

Cheung, F. M., & Lau, B. W. (1982). Situational variations of help-seeking behavior among Chinese patients. *Comprehensive Psychiatry, 23,* 252–262.

Chun, C.-A., Enomoto, K., & Sue, S. (1996). Health care issues among Asian Americans: Implications of somatization. In P. M. Kato & T. Mann (Eds.), *Handbook of diversity issues in health psychology* (pp. 439–467). New York, NY: Plenum Press.

Corrigan, P. (2004). How stigma interferes with mental health care. *American Psychologist, 59*(7), 614–625.

Hardy, K. V., & Laszloffy, T. A. (1995). The cultural genogram: Key to training culturally competent family therapists. *Journal of Marital and Family Therapy, 21*(3), 227–237.

Hoeffel, E. M., Rastogi, S., Kim, M. O., & Shahid, H. (2012). *The Asian population: 2010.* 2010 Census briefs (Report no. C2010BR-11, pp. 1–23). Washington, DC: U.S. Census Bureau.

Hu, T. W., Snowden, L. R., Jerrell, J. M., & Nguyen, T. D. (1991). Ethnic populations in public mental health: Services choice and level of use. *American Journal of Public Health, 81,* 1429–1434.

Hwang, W. (2006a). Acculturative family distancing: Theory, research, and clinical practice. *Psychotherapy: Theory, Research, Practice, Training, 43*(4), 397–409.

Hwang, W. (2006b). The Psychotherapy Adaptation and Modification Framework (PAMF): Application to Asian Americans. *American Psychologist, 67*(7), 702–715.

Hwang, W. (2009). The Formative Method for Adapting Psychotherapy (FMAP): A community-based developmental approach to culturally adapting therapy. *Professional Psychology: Research and Practice, 40*(4), 369–377.

Hwang, W., & Wood, J. J. (2009). Acculturative Family Distancing (AFD) in immigrant families: A structural model of linkages with mental health outcomes among young adults. *Child Psychiatry & Human Development, 40,* 123–138.

Hwang, W., Wood, J. J., & Fujimoto, K. (2010). Acculturative Family Distancing (AFD) and depression in Chinese American families. *Journal of Consulting and Clinical Psychology*, 78(5), 655–677.

Lee, E. (1997). Overview: The assessment and treatment of Asian American families. In E. Lee (Ed.), *Working with Asian Americans: A guide for clinician* (pp. 3–37). New York, NY: Guilford Press.

Lin, T. Y., & Lin, M. C. (1978). Service delivery issues in Asian–North American communities. *American Journal of Psychiatry, 135,* 454–456.

Lo, H., & Fung, K. P. (2003). Culturally competent psychotherapy. *Canadian Journal of Psychiatry, 48*(3), 161–170.

Meyer, O. L., Zane, N., Cho, Y., & Takeuchi, D. T. (2009). Use of specialty mental health services by Asian Americans with psychiatric disorders. *Journal of Consulting and Clinical Psychology, 77,* 1000–1005.

Miranda, J., Bernal, G., Lau, A., Kohn, L., Hwang, W., & La Framboise, T. (2005). State of the science on psychosocial interventions for ethnic minorities. *Annual Review of Clinical Psychology, 1,* 113–142.

Nagayama-Hall, G. C. (2001). Psychotherapy research with ethnic minorities: Empirical, ethical, and conceptual issues. *Journal of Consulting and Clinical Psychology, 69*(3), 502–510.

Snowden, L. R., & Cheung, F. K. (1990). Use of inpatient mental health services by members of ethnic minority groups. *American Psychologist, 45,* 347–355.

Sue, D. W. (1982). Position paper: Cross-cultural counseling competencies. *Counseling Psychologist, 10*(2), 45–52.

Sue, D. W., Arredondo, P., & McDavis, R. J. (1992). Multicultural counseling competencies and standards: A call to the profession. *Journal of Multicultural Counseling & Development, 20*(2), 64–88.

Sue, D. W., & Sue, S. (1987). Cultural factors in the clinical assessment of Asian Americans. *Journal of Consulting & Clinical Psychology, 55*(4), 479–487.

Sue, S. (1977). Community mental health services to minority groups: Some optimism, some pessimism. *American Psychologist, 32,* 616–624.

Sue, S. (1998). In search of cultural competence in psychotherapy and counseling. *American Psychologist, 53*(4), 440–448.

Sue, S., Zane, N., Hall, G. C. N., & Berger, L. K. (2009). The case for cultural competency in psychotherapeutic interventions. *Annual Review of Psychology, 60*, 525–548.

Task Force on Promotion and Dissemination of Psychological Procedures. (1995). Training in and dissemination of empirically-validated psychological treatments: Report and recommendations. *Clinical Psychologist, 48*, 3–23.

Zane, N., Enomoto, K., & Chun, C. (1994). Treatment outcomes of Asian- and White-American clients in outpatient therapy. *Journal of Community Psychology, 22*, 177–191.

2

Treating Depression in Asian American Adults

WEI-CHIN HWANG

The Surgeon General's report "Mental Health: Culture, Race, and Ethnicity" noted that provision of services to Asian Americans is complicated because of linguistic and cultural challenges (U.S. Department of Health and Human Services [USDHHS], 2001). Specifically, more than half of Asian Americans who may need treatment require linguistic and culturally competent services. In addition, a number of other factors, such as concrete barriers (e.g., lack of finances and health insurance) and cultural barriers (e.g., stigma, misperception, cultural stereotypes, and cultural incongruity), have resulted in underutilization of mental health services by Asian Americans (Cheung & Snowden, 1990; Lin & Lin, 1978; Snowden & Cheung, 1990; Sue, 1977; Sue & Sue, 2003). Given that the mental health needs and rates of illness for Asian Americans are similar to those of other Americans (USDHHS, 2001), figuring out how to best provide services in an effective way is an important endeavor. Moreover, there have been no rigorously conducted mental health treatment outcome studies (i.e., randomized controlled trials) conducted on this understudied group. As a result, it is still unclear whether Western-oriented therapies are effective in treating depressed Asian Americans and whether culturally modifying treatments will improve outcomes and reduce dropouts (Hwang, 2006).

Are Asian Americans truly a model minority, and, as such, do they really experience few problems and have no need for mental health services? As noted in the introductory chapter, Asian Americans are very diverse in terms of country of origin, socioeconomic status, migration status (e.g., voluntary, involuntary, undocumented), pre- and postmigration factors, and immigration cohorts. It is important that treatment providers avoid stereotyping clients and understand the heterogeneity within Asian Americans. Available evidence suggests that Asian Americans do not experience fewer mental health difficulties than other Americans, although the distributions of problems may be different (USDHHS, 2001). In relation to depression, the evidence is mixed, with some preliminary findings suggesting that diagnosable depression is lower among Asian Americans than among other Americans but higher than Asians in Asia (Chen et al., 1993; Hwang, Myers, & Takeuchi, 2000; Hwu, Yeh, & Chang, 1989; Kessler et al., 1994; Takeuchi et al., 1998). In contrast, most research on severity of distress and depressive symptoms reveals greater difficulties among Asian Americans than among White Americans (Hurh & Kim, 1990; Kuo, 1984; Ying, 1988). Cultural differences in communication and expression of distress (Hwang, Wood, Lin, & Cheung, 2005), variations in psychiatric illness manifestations (e.g., culturally specific idioms of distress or culture-bound syndromes; Hall & Yee, 2012; Sue, Cheng, Saad, & Chu, 2012), and the community's differential response to epidemiological research methods (e.g., because stigma toward mental illness is high in Asian culture, Asian Americans may be less responsive to talking about personal problems with people whom they do not know).

Why do Asian Americans become depressed? As with other groups, common factors such stress, family conflict, lack of family support, poor physical health, and prior individual or family psychiatric history have been found to increase risk for depression in multiple Asian groups (Chung & Kagawa-Singer, 1993; Hurh & Kim,

1990; Hwang et al., 2000; Lin, Tazuma, & Masuda, 1979; Takeuchi et al., 1998). In addition, a number of culture-related factors also seem to increase risk for depression, including acculturative stress, level of acculturation, difficulties forming a cohesive ethnic identity, and disconnect from social networks and supports (Hwang, Chun, Takeuchi, Myers, & Siddarth, 2005; Kuo & Tsai, 1986; Oh, Koeske, & Sales, 2002; Phinney, Horenczyk, Liebkind, & Vedder, 2001; Williams & Berry, 1991).

What are some of the difficulties associated with treating depressed Asian Americans? Because Asian Americans tend to underutilize services and delay seeking help, they are more likely to be more severely depressed when they do seek help (Lin & Lin, 1978; Sue, 1977; Sue & Sue, 1987; Ting & Hwang, 2009). That is, they are likely to have turned to mental health services after exhausting their individual coping and support resources. This is particularly true of less acculturated Asian Americans, who may have little exposure to mental illness and its treatment, and where cultural stereotypes about those being mentally ill being "crazy" or "weak" are widespread (Hwang, 2006).

Do Western therapies have clinical utility for Asian Americans? Other than naturalistic research that uses distal measures of outcome, there is currently very little research examining how Asian Americans react to mental health treatment. However, the available evidence suggests that Asian Americans are more likely to drop out of treatment prematurely, evidence less therapeutic progress, and be less satisfied with treatment (Sue, 1977; Sue, Fujino, Hu, & Takeuchi, 1991; Zane, Enomoto, & Chun, 1994). The current literature is limited because no randomized controlled trials have examined the treatment progress of depressed Asian Americans using empirically supported treatments (Miranda et al., 2005). As a result, it is not clear to what extent psychotherapy is beneficial for Asian Americans, which therapies (e.g., cognitive or interpersonal) are likely to work best, and whether cultural modifications or adaptations to traditional therapies will improve results (Hwang, 2006, 2009; Hwang, Wood, Lin, &

Cheung, 2006). Hall, Hong, Zane, and Meyer (2011) have suggested that certain treatments, such as mindfulness and acceptance-based psychotherapies, may already be more culturally aligned with Asian culture and might serve as a good starting point for cultural adaptations. Hwang (2006, 2009) has developed bottom-up and top-down frameworks for culturally adapting psychotherapy (see Chapter 1) and is currently conducting a clinical trial testing the effectiveness of CBT versus culturally adapted CBT (Hwang, 2008a, 2008b). No matter which theoretical orientation is chosen, great care needs to be taken not to overly stereotype and to take into account the complex interplay between clinical and cultural issues (Hwang, 2011).

Because Asian Americans are so diverse and vary in acculturative levels, no one set of recommendations will accommodate and generalize to all members of this heterogeneous group of people. Sue (1998) cautioned that mental health practitioners need to take into consideration the principle of dynamic sizing. Specifically, when applying cultural knowledge clinically, therapists need to learn how to flexibly apply cultural knowledge so that treatments can be individualized and rigid overgeneralizations minimized. In addition, it is also important to remember that practitioners are not just treating an Asian American, but that Asian Americans have multiple aspects to their identity. Hays (2001) highlighted the importance of understanding cultural complexities in her ADDRESSING framework when treating ethnic minorities. She notes that that a client's (A) age and generational influences, (D) developmental or acquired disabilities (D), (R) religion and spiritual orientation, (E) ethnicity, (S) socioeconomic status, (S) sexual orientation, (I) indigenous heritage, (N) national origin, and (G) gender should all be considered in treating that client (e.g., one would treat a Vietnamese American gay male who is highly acculturated very differently from a Vietnamese American heterosexual female who is a recent refugee from Cambodia).

Practitioners using recommendations from this chapter should take dynamic sizing and cultural complexities to heart, as recommendations provided are general and target Asian Americans who are less acculturated. Here, I outline recommendations and discuss issues involved in treating a single, 35-year-old, Chinese American woman. Ms. K grew up in mainland China and immigrated to the United States in her early 20s. She spoke little English, and therapy was conducted in Mandarin Chinese. She came into treatment presenting with symptoms of depression, such as hopelessness, suicidal ideation, and insomnia, that were increasingly affecting her functioning and ability to work. She had no previous experience of psychotherapy and felt extremely uncomfortable coming into the clinic for treatment. She was also worried about privacy and confidentiality issues. These recommendations target several areas, including orienting clients to therapy, accurately conceptualizing the problem, and designing an effective treatment plan that is framed in a culturally compatible manner with the client (Hwang, 2006).

Therapy Orientation

When treating depressed Asian adults such as Ms. K, it is important to orient them to therapy. Although traditional clinical perspectives affirm the importance of providing therapy orientations to clients, in practice, therapists working from different theoretical orientations and disciplines orient clients to varying degrees. Acosta, Yamamoto, Evans, and Skilbeck (1983) found that Latino, African American, and Caucasian psychiatric clients who underwent therapy orientation prior to their first therapy session felt more knowledgeable and positive toward psychotherapy. Because psychotherapy is culturally foreign to many Asian Americans, they are also likely to benefit from therapy orientation, which helps demystify it and prepare clients for therapy (Hwang, 2006). When working with less acculturated Asian American adults, therapy orientations become even more critical for a number of reasons. First, many Asian Americans have had little exposure to mental health and its treatment. Cultural stereotypes of those who are mentally ill being "crazy" or "weak" increase the amount of stigma and shame that depressed Asian Americans may feel. This increases the likelihood that Asian Americans will not come to treatment at all or will delay treatment until their problems become intolerably worse (Ting & Hwang, 2009). Ensuring confidentiality and privacy, as well as reducing the stigma of psychotherapy, was emphasized in the earlier sessions of treatment with Ms. K. Because of delays in treatment and similar to Ms. K, many Asian Americans seeking help for depression come in experiencing hopelessness and suicidal ideation that should be carefully monitored.

When orienting clients for treatment, it is important to elucidate the structure of therapy (e.g., what is a therapy hour, how often should they come in for treatment), the roles of both the client and therapist (e.g., how clients and therapists commonly behave and the extent to which both parties do the talking), common Asian American reactions to beginning therapy (e.g., feeling awkward, having difficulty expressing oneself and talking about one's problems to a stranger, that sometimes clients feel worse before they feel better, desires to drop out of treatment prematurely because they do not feel they are getting better fast enough, and wanting to drop out of treatment because they are temporarily feeling better), and common questions that Asian American clients have but may not proactively ask (e.g., how many sessions will it take before one starts feeling better, how does therapy work, what specific techniques will be used); to normalize feelings (e.g., feelings of shame, embarrassment, and weakness associated with stigma); and to affirm to clients that they are doing the right thing (e.g., it takes a lot of courage and strength to take the steps necessary to improve one's problems; Hwang, 2006, 2009). Of course, not all of these goals can be accomplished in the first session, especially when Asian Americans are more likely to enter treatment more severely depressed or in a state of crisis. However, addressing these issues early in treatment may reduce the chances of premature treatment failure and help position the client to make the most of therapy.

Asian cultures place great importance on social relationships, hierarchical relations, and respect for authority (Lin, 2001; Zhang et al., 2002). When treating less acculturated Asian Americans, it is important for the therapist to take an authoritative stance because of cultural expectations that treatment providers are expert authority figures who can help them solve their problems (Hwang, 2006; Lin, 2001; Zhang et al., 2002). Therapists who do not take an authoritative stance early in therapy may be at risk for losing their clients' faith in the therapist and the treatment, especially in that Asian Americans tend to be more severely ill when they do seek treatment and may expect direct advice, more structure, problem solving, and immediate symptom improvement (Lin & Lin, 1978; Sue, 1977; Sue & Sue, 1987).

Problem Conceptualization

To develop an accurate understanding of the client's presenting problems, therapists need to be attuned to cultural differences in the expression of distress and what clients believe to be the cause of their problem (Hwang, 2006). For example, although Ms. K presents with classic symptoms of depression (e.g., hopelessness, insomnia, and suicidal ideation), there may be cultural differences in how the client communicates this distress to the therapist and in the timing of this communication. Many Asian immigrants come from cultures that place a greater emphasis on high-context communication (e.g., use of more nonverbal, verbally indirect, and restrained communication) than low-context communication (e.g., more verbally direct and expressive; Hall, 1976; Hwang, 2006; Lee, 1997). Practitioners also need to be aware of cultural differences in nonverbal communication styles that may be more salient in Asian cultures, including proxemics (the use and perception of interpersonal space), kinesics (bodily movements and facial expressions), and paralanguage (vocal cues such as pauses, silences, and inflections; Sue, 1990). For example, Ms. K often expressed her depression somatically and complained of headaches and bodily aches and pains. Moreover, instead of stating how sad she was, she expressed her distress by presenting with low energy and keeping her head lowered with little eye contact. Practitioners who do not understand cultural differences in communication might misinterpret her symptoms for being aloof or uninterested in treatment. In addition, cultural norms in how much one reveals private information to a stranger and how comfortable one is talking about one's problems may impact how much clients such as Ms. K feel open at the beginning of treatment and the degree to which that comfort increases or decreases as the therapeutic relationship develops.

Awareness of ethnic differences in expression of distress can also improve diagnostic accuracy (Hwang, Myers, Abe-Kim, & Ting, 2008). There is an established body of literature suggesting that Asians are more likely to express somatic forms of depression, which are believed to be more culturally acceptable and less stigmatizing (Chun, Enomoto, & Sue, 1996; Kleinman & Kleinman, 1985). Cultural manifestations of somatic depression such as neurasthenia or "nerve weakness" that are more culturally acceptable and less stigmatizing have also been documented (Kleinman, 1985; Zheng et al., 1997). Treatment plans that target physical complaints may be beneficial. For example, physical exercise and healthy activities were implemented as a behavioral activation strategy in Ms. K's treatment. However, this does not mean that Asian immigrants do not experience emotional and cognitive symptoms. Even though some may be more likely to focus on physical complaints when they initially come in to treatment, it is important not to stereotype Asian Americans because most are fully aware and capable of expressing their feelings and talking about their problems, especially after a working relationship is developed (Cheung, 1985; Cheung & Lau, 1982). The therapist was very patient with Ms. K and helped her feel more comfortable in treatment. As a result, Ms. K began to talk more about her feelings, began to reveal more of her negative internal dialogue, and became more open to discussing the stressors in her life. Accurate understanding of how the client communicates and expresses her distress is very important if the practitioner is to accurately diagnose and understand her problems (Hwang et al., 2008).

Treatment Plan and Therapeutic Techniques

After a grounded understanding of the client's problems is achieved and the factors that caused and sustained them are identified, a culturally informed treatment plan can be developed (Hwang, 2006; Hwang et al., 2008). This treatment plan should contain the client's specific goals for therapy and identify what therapeutic techniques and activities will help the client and therapist reach their objectives. Therapeutic goals and the techniques used to achieve them should be consistent with how clients experience their problems and what they believe caused them, also known as the client's explanatory model of illness (Kleinman, 1978). For example, if Ms. K comes into treatment reporting feelings of depression exacerbated by a number of stressors, the initial treatment plan might target reduction of depressive symptoms through various therapeutic techniques, such as stress management, cognitive reframing, and skills building through role-playing (Hwang et al., 2006). If the client believes her problem is somatic and caused by an imbalance or stagnation of positive qi, or energy, the therapist might prescribe behavioral activation exercises, teach progressive muscle relaxation and deep breathing skills, and encourage her to join various social activities that target helping the client achieve a positive balance in energy. This knowledge was integrated into Ms. K's treatment plan. She was also asked to sit in the sun and meditate as a way to cultivate her yang qi (male, positive, or sunlight energy) because in Chinese medicine, depression is related to too much yin qi (female, negative, or lunar energy). If the practitioner's explanatory model is different from that of the client's, and the practitioner believes the client's somatic symptoms are caused by maladaptive cognitions, the therapist can still help the client replace maladaptive cognitions with coping thoughts by explaining to the client that sometimes negative thinking can also cause an imbalance in qi and lead to problematic bodily symptoms. The takeaway point is that the practitioner needs to bridge the client's and therapist's explanatory models and explain how the treatment plan will help her reach their common goals.

Cultural bridging—relating psychotherapeutic concepts to Asian cultural beliefs and practices—is an important skill to implement if the practitioner wants to more fully engage the client and gain their buy-in and adherence to treatment (Ham, 1989; Hong, 1993; Hwang, 2006). This requires that the therapist be familiar with the client's background. For example, CBT principles of relaxation training can be bridged to Chinese cultural traditions (e.g., traditional Chinese medicine [TCM], meditation, qi-gong [a meditative practice that focuses on energy and breathing], and tai qi quan [a Chinese martial arts form that focus on qi or energy]) that are believed to improve mental and physical health through a balance of yin and yang (negative and positive energies). Establishing cultural bridges early in treatment may also reduce the cultural shock clients feel when participating in treatments that are culturally foreign and unfamiliar. Ideally, these bridges should be used to link the client's explanatory model for their problems and the therapeutic techniques used to address them, such as strategies that simultaneously focus on the mind and body, because Asian culture places heavier emphasis on this balance (Hwang, 2006; Hwang, Wood, Lin, & Cheung, 2006).

Drawing links and using culturally familiar terms and values can also increase feelings of comfort, give treatment more meaning, and increase treatment adherence (Hwang, 2006, 2008a). For example, in working with Ms. K, the therapist could make a metaphorical link between the client's life experiences, current level of hopelessness, and the resilience of Asian bamboo in facing adversity. Specifically, like bamboo, life can have many twists and turns, but if one can take a step back and look at the bigger picture, one has a better perspective on how to best shape one's future and the direction of one's life, what Confucius would call the "right path" or to be of "right mind" (Hwang, 2006, 2008a). Drawing a link between Chinese four-word metaphorical sayings known as *Chengyu*, which are used to teach ethical and moral principles in Chinese culture, to therapeutic principles may help bridge therapeutic concepts to the cultural background of the client (Hwang et al., 2006). *Shuang guan ji xia* means literally two brushes painting together and refers to the story of a famous artist who painted using two brushes in one hand simultaneously (Hong, 1987). This story could facilitate understanding and simultaneous engagement of two core CBT principles: challenging maladaptive cognitions and replacing them with coping thoughts and engaging in behavioral strategies such as exercise and meditation to improve depressed mood.

Conclusion

In summary, psychotherapy can be an effective method for treating depression in Asian American adults. Unfortunately, there continues to be a dearth of empirical literature examining how Asian Americans respond to mental health treatment. What little research there is suggests that Asian Americans are more likely to drop out of treatment prematurely and evidence less therapeutic progress than other groups. Until this research gap is filled, our understanding of how well Asian Americans respond to psychotherapy and how to improve treatment outcomes will continue to be limited. In the meantime, there are a number of practices that providers can provide to improve care, such as orienting clients to therapy and using cultural bridges and metaphors to make psychotherapy understandable and accessible.

References

Acosta, F. X., Yamamoto, J., Evans, L. A., & Skilbeck, W. M. (1983). Preparing low-income Latinos, Black, and White patients for psychotherapy: Evaluation of a new orientation program. *Journal of Clinical Psychology, 39*(6), 872–877.

Chen, C. N., Wong, J., Lee, N., Chan-Ho, M. W., Lau, J. T., & Fung, M. (1993). The Shatin community mental health survey in Hong Kong II: Major findings. *Archives of General Psychiatry, 50,* 125–133.

Cheung, F. M. (1985). An overview of psychopathology in Hong Kong with special reference to somatic presentation. In W. S. Tseng & D. Wu (Eds.), *Chinese culture and mental health* (pp. 287–300). Orlando, FL: Academic Press.

Cheung, F. M., & Lau, B. W. (1982). Situational variations of help-seeking behavior among Chinese patients. *Comprehensive Psychiatry, 23,* 252–262.

Cheung, F. K., & Snowden, L. R. (1990). Community mental health and ethnic minority populations. *Community Mental Health Journal, 26,* 277–291.

Chun, C.-A., Enomoto, K., & Sue, S. (1996). Health care issues among Asian Americans: Implications of somatization. In P. M. Kato & T. Mann (Eds.), *Handbook of diversity issues in health psychology* (pp. 439–467). New York, NY: Plenum Press.

Chung, R. C., & Kagawa-Singer, M. (1993). Predictors of psychological distress among Southeast Asian refugees. *Social Science and Medicine, 36,* 631–639.

Hall, E. T. (1976). *Beyond culture.* New York, NY: Anchor Press.

Hall, G. C. N., Hong, J. J., Zane, N. W. S., & Meyer, O. L. (2011). Culturally competent treatment for Asian Americans: The relevance of mindfulness and acceptance-based psychotherapies. *Clinical Psychology: Science and Practice, 18*(3), 215–231.

Hall, G. C. N., & Yee, A. H. (2012). U.S. mental health policy: Addressing the neglect of Asian Americans. *Asian American Journal of Psychology, 3,* 181–193.

Ham, M. D. (Ed.). (1989). Empathic understanding: A skill for "joining" with immigrant families. *Journal of Strategic and Systemic Therapies, 8*(2), 36–40.

Hays, P. (2001). *Addressing cultural complexities in practice: A framework for clinicians and counselors.* Washington, DC: American Psychological Association.

Hong, G. K. (1993). Synthesizing Eastern and Western psychotherapeutic approaches: Contextual factors in psychotherapy with Asian Americans. In J. L. Chin, J. L. Liem, M. D. Ham, & G. K. Hong (Eds.), *Transference and empathy in Asian American psychotherapy: Cultural values and treatment needs* (pp. 77–90). Westport, CT: Praeger.

Hong, Y. N. (1987). *Chinese saying told in pictures.* Taipei, Taiwan: Sinora Magazine.

Hurh, W. M., & Kim, K. C. (1990). Correlates of Korean immigrants' mental health. *Journal of Nervous and Mental Disease, 178,* 703–711.

Hwang, W. (2006). The Psychotherapy Adaptation and Modification Framework (PAMF): Application to Asian Americans. *American Psychologist, 67*(7), 702–715.

Hwang, W. (2008a). *Improving your mood: A culturally responsive and holistic approach to treating depression in Chinese Americans* (Client manual—Chinese and English versions). Unpublished copyrighted treatment manual.

Hwang, W. (2008b). *Improving your mood: A culturally responsive and holistic approach to treating depression in Chinese Americans* (Therapist manual—Chinese and English versions). Unpublished copyrighted training manual.

Hwang, W. (2009). The Formative Method for Adapting Psychotherapy (FMAP): A community-based developmental approach to culturally adapting therapy. *Professional Psychology: Research and Practice, 40*(4), 369–377.

Hwang, W. (2011). Cultural adaptations: A complex interplay between clinical and cultural issues. *Clinical Psychology: Science and Practice, 18*(3), 238–241.

Hwang, W., Chun, C., Takeuchi, D. T., Myers, H. F., & Siddarth, P. (2005). Age of first-onset major depression in Chinese Americans. *Cultural Diversity and Ethnic Minority Psychology, 11*(1), 16–27.

Hwang, W., Myers, H. F., Abe-Kim, J., &.Ting, J. (2008). A conceptual paradigm for understanding culture's impact on mental health: The cultural influences on mental health (CIMH) model. *Clinical Psychology Review, 28,* 211–227.

Hwang, W., Myers, H. F., & Takeuchi, D. T. (2000). Psychosocial predictors of first-onset depression in Chinese Americans. *Social Psychiatry and Psychiatric Epidemiology, 35*, 133–145.

Hwang, W., Wood, J. J., Lin, K., & Cheung, F. (2006). Cognitive-behavioral therapy with Chinese Americans: Research, theory, and clinical practice. *Cognitive and Behavioral Practice, 13*, 293–303.

Hwu, H., Yeh, E., & Chang, L. (1989). Prevalence of psychiatric disorders in Taiwan defined by the Chinese Diagnostic Interview Schedule. *Acta Psychiatra Scandinavia, 79*, 136–47.

Kessler, R. C., McGonagle, K. A., Zhao, S., Nelson, C. B., Hughes, M., Eshleman, S.,...Kendler, K. S. (1994). Lifetime and 12-month prevalence of DSM-III-R psychiatric disorders in the United States. *Archives of General Psychiatry, 51*, 8–19.

Kleinman, A. (1978). Clinical relevance of anthropological and cross-cultural research: Concepts and strategies. *American Journal of Psychiatry, 135*(4), 427–431.

Kleinman, A., & Kleinman, J. (1985). Somatization: The interconnections in Chinese society among culture, depressive experiences, and the meanings of pain. In A. Kleinman & B. J. Good (Eds.), *Culture and depression: Studies in the anthropology and cross-cultural psychiatry of affect and disorder* (pp. 429–490). Berkeley, CA: University of California Press.

Kuo, W. (1984). Prevalence of depression among Asian-Americans. *Journal of Nervous & Mental Disease, 172*(8), 449–457.

Kuo, W., & Tsai, Y. (1986). Social networking, hardiness and immigrant's mental health. *Journal of Health & Social Behavior, 27*(2), 133–149.

Lee, E. (1997). Overview: The assessment and treatment of Asian American families. In E. Lee (Ed.), *Working with Asian Americans: A guide for clinicians* (pp. 3-37). New York, NY: Guilford Press.

Lin, K., Tazuma, L., & Masuda, M. (1979). Adaptational problems of Vietnamese refugees Part 1: Health and mental health status. *Archives of General Psychiatry, 36*(9), 955–961.

Lin, T. Y., & Lin, M. C. (1978). Service delivery issues in Asian–North American communities. *American Journal of Psychiatry, 135*, 454–456.

Lin, Y.-N. (2001). The application of cognitive-behavioral therapy to counseling Chinese. *American Journal of Psychotherapy, 55*(4), 46–58.

Miranda, J., Bernal, G., Lau, A., Kohn, L., Hwang, W., & La Framboise, T. (2005). State of the science on psychosocial interventions for ethnic minorities. *Annual Review of Clinical Psychology, 1*, 113–142.

Oh, Y., Koeske, G. F., & Sales, E. (2002). Acculturation, stress, and depressive symptoms among Korean immigrants in the United States. *Journal of Social Psychology, 142*(4), 511–526.

Phinney, J. S., Horenczyk, G., Liebkind, K., & Vedder, P. (2001). Ethnic identity, immigration, and well-being: An interactional perspective. *Journal of Social Issues, 57*(3), 493–510.

Snowden, L. R., & Cheung, F. K. (1990). Use of inpatient mental health services by members of ethnic minority groups. *American Psychologist, 45*, 347–355.

Sue, D. W. (1990). Culture-specific strategies in counseling: A conceptual framework. *Professional Psychology: Research & Practice, 21*(6), 424–433.

Sue, D. W., & Sue, S. (1987). Cultural factors in the clinical assessment of Asian Americans. *Journal of Consulting & Clinical Psychology, 55*(4), 479–487.

Sue, D. W., & Sue, S. (2003). *Counseling the culturally diverse: Theory and practice*. Hoboken, NJ: John Wiley & Sons.

Sue, S. (1977). Community mental health services to minority groups: Some optimism, some pessimism. *American Psychologist, 32*, 616–624.

Sue, S. (1998). In search of cultural competence in psychotherapy and counseling. *American Psychologist, 53*(4), 440–448.

Sue, S., Cheng, J. K. Y., Saad, C. S., & Chu, J. P. (2012). Asian American mental health: A call to action. *American Psychologist, 67*, 532–544.

Sue, S., Fujino, D. C., Hu, L., & Takeuchi, D. T., (1991). Community mental health services for ethnic minority groups: A test of the cultural responsiveness hypothesis. *Journal of Consulting & Clinical Psychology, 59*(4), 533–540.

Takeuchi, D. T., Chung, R. C., Lin, K. M., Shen, H., Kurasaki, K., Chun, C., & Sue, S. (1998). Lifetime and twelve-month prevalence rates of major depressive episodes and dysthymia among Chinese Americans in Los Angeles. *American Journal of Psychiatry, 155*, 1407–1414.

Ting, J. Y., & Hwang, W. (2009). Cultural influences on help-seeking attitudes in Asian American students. *American Journal of Orthopsychiatry, 79*, 125–132.

U.S. Department of Health and Human Services. (2001). *Mental health: Culture, race, and ethnicity—A supplement to mental* health: A report of the Surgeon General. Rockville, MD: U.S. Department of Health and Human Services, Public Health Service, Office of the Surgeon General.

Williams, C. L., & Berry, J. W. (1991). Primary prevention of acculturative stress among refugees: Application of psychological theory and practice. American Psychologist, 46(6), 632–641.

Ying, Y. (1988). Depressive symptomatology among Chinese-Americans as measured by the CES-D. Journal of Clinical Psychology, 44, 739–746.

Zane, N., Enomoto, K., & Chun, C. (1994). Treatment outcomes of Asian- and White-American clients in outpatient therapy. Journal of Community Psychology, 22, 177–191.

Zhang, Y., Young, D., Lee, S., Li, L., Zhang, H., Xiao, Z.,...Chang, D. F. (2002). Chinese Taoist cognitive psychotherapy in the treatment of generalized anxiety disorder in contemporary China. Transcultural Psychiatry, 39(1), 115–129.

Zheng, Y. P., Lin, K. M., Takeuchi, D. T., Kurasaki, K. S., Wang, Y., & Cheung, F. (1997). An epidemiological study of neurasthenia in Chinese-Americans in Los Angeles. Comprehensive Psychiatry, 38(5), 249–259.

3

Depression among Asian and Pacific Islander American Elders

DONNA K. NAGATA, AMY H. TSAI-CHAE, AND TERESA U. NGUYEN

Historical Overview of Asian American Elders

Asian and Pacific Islander Americans (APIA) are the fastest growing minority group in the United States (Hoeffel, Rastogi, Kim, & Shahid, 2012). Consequently, it is vital that professionals and researchers gain a better awareness of the mental health needs of these populations across the lifespan, including older adulthood. In 2011, 21.0% of persons age 65 and older in the United States were ethnic minorities, and APIA constituted about 4% of this group (Administration on Aging; AoA, 2012). Between 2000 and 2010, the older population (those 65 and older) increased at a faster rate (15.1%) than the total population (9.7%; Werner, 2011). The percentage of APIA elders within that older group is expected to increase significantly in the future. Whereas the European American older population is projected to increase by 54% between 2012 and 2030, the APIA older population is projected to increase by 119% (AoA, 2012).

From an outsider's perspective, APIA older adults are often invisible, with little attention paid to their mental health needs. Part of this neglect stems from idealized assumptions that stereotype APIA elders as members of a "model minority" group who receive extensive family support in their later life (Casado & Leung, 2001; Sakauye, 1992). Older APIA adults also tend to be viewed as a homogeneous group, even though the term *Asian American and Pacific Islander* represents any one of more than 25 ethnic groups, each with its own language, immigration history, and distinct cultural values (Iwamasa & Hilliard, 1999). For example, in addition to the ethnic categories of Chinese, Filipino, Korean, Vietnamese, Japanese, and Cambodian, the Native Hawaiian and Pacific Islander categories include multiple Polynesian, Micronesian, and Melanesian populations that have diverse cultures and languages, such as Native Hawaiian, Samoan, Guamanian, Chamarro, Fijian, Chuukese, Tahitian, Tongan, and Tokelauan (Hixson, Hepler, & Kim, 2012). The vast diversity among APIA is evident even if one focuses on the single dimension of language. Although more APIA speak Chinese than any of the other Asian languages, Chinese has hundreds of dialects with distinct differences in pronunciation that can be mutually unintelligible across subgroups. There are also two main forms of Chinese written language, with the simplified form predominantly used in mainland China and a traditional form predominantly used in Taiwan and Hong Kong. Furthermore, the range of acculturation levels within each ethnic and cultural group poses additional challenges for mental health researchers and practitioners. Some older Chinese Americans may be the third generation of their family in the United States, and other Chinese American elders may be recent immigrants. Some foreign-born elders may have retained the citizenship of their home country, and others may be naturalized citizens. According to the 2010 American Community Survey from the U.S. Census Bureau (Grieco et al., 2012), 28% of the nation's nearly 40 million foreign-born residents were born in Asia. The Asian-born population was found to have the second highest naturalized citizenship rates among foreign-born groups (58%). Clearly, the life contexts for APIA elders can vary considerably.

The heterogeneity among APIA older adults is also reflected in their diverse immigration histories. Large numbers of Vietnamese first came to the United States as war refugees in the 1970s; the earliest Chinese were recruited as laborers in the mid-1890s (Zane, Morton, Chu, & Lin, 2004). Adding to this complexity is the fact that there are often different waves of immigration within a single Asian ethnic group. Toarmino and Chun (1997), for example, described three waves of Korean immigration that occurred between the early 1880s and the late 1960s. Each wave had unique preimmigration sociodemographic characteristics and postimmigration patterns of settlement, and each encountered different sociopolitical contexts within the United States.

As a visible minority group, Asian Americans have long been the targets of stereotypes and discrimination (Sue, 1991). Throughout the history of Asian immigration to the United States, there have been anti-Asian restrictions. In the 1800s, for example, when it was convenient and desirable for Asians to enter the country, large numbers of Chinese and Japanese were recruited to work as farmers, railroad builders, and factory workers (Takaki, 1989; True & Guillermo, 1996). However, as the need for Asian laborers passed, laws were enacted that restricted or halted Asian immigration and focused on segregating and outlawing their naturalization (for a summary of these laws, see Kitano & Daniels, 1995; Young & Takeuchi, 1998). Furthermore, historical traumas experienced by specific groups of APIA elders, such as the mass incarceration of Japanese Americans during World War II[1] and the violence experienced by Korean American store owners during the Rodney King riots in Los Angeles, may have long-term impacts on their current psychological status (e.g., Nagata, 1998). Such negative past history has potentially harmful effects on these elders' subjective well-being. At the same time, there are APIA elder refugees who came to the United States fleeing genocide and political or economic crises. Their histories add further to the range of diversity among the group included under the umbrella term *APIA elders*.

Educational and economic resources also vary significantly across APIA. Though some Asian ethnic elders have resources similar to those reported for non-Hispanic European Americans in the United States, the majority do not. In 1999, Wykle and Ford reported that Hawaiian (28%), Samoan (25%), and Chinese (24%) elders had about the same level of educational attainment as the general population of U.S. older adults (28%), whereas older Japanese Americans (38%) had a higher proportion of high school graduates. However, Hmong (2%), Cambodian and Laotian (7% each), Thai (11%), and Guamanian (12%) older adults had significantly lower formal education levels than U.S. older adults and other Asian groups. A similar split in distribution between East Asians and Southeast Asians was observed in data on poverty rates, labor-market-sector participation, and access to types of health insurance (Wykle & Ford, 1999).

Despite an increase in the number of studies on the mental health of APIA more generally, literature on the mental health of older APIA remains sparse. There have been only a handful of extensive reviews on the mental health of older Asian American adults (Browne, Fong, & Mokuau, 1994; Iwamasa & Hilliard, 1999; Iwamasa & Sorocco, 2007; Trinh & Ahmed, 2009). Furthermore, most studies of this population focus on larger APIA populations, such as Chinese or Korean older adults, or on populations with earlier immigration histories, such as Japanese Americans. Studies on Pacific Islander older adults, by contrast, are rare. Given that there is little research for each specific ethnic group, this chapter presents summaries from research conducted with a variety of APIA ethnic groups with a word of caution against generalizing the findings for a particular APIA group to other Asian ethnic groups.

Prevalence and Risk Factors

A range of studies have examined depression generally among APIA groups without a specific focus on elders. Flaskerud and Hu

(1992) reported that depression was the most frequent diagnosis given to Asian clients who obtained services at Los Angeles County mental health facilities. Additional studies have reported equivalent or higher rates of depression among Chinese, Japanese, and Korean Americans than among European Americans (Aldwin & Greenberger, 1987; Hymes & Akiyama, 1991; Lam, Pacala, & Smith, 1997; Yeung et al., 2004; Ying, 1988). Yeung et al. (2004) found an overall prevalence rate of 19.6% for depression among Chinese American primary care patients in Boston, Massachusetts. This rate was much higher than the 5 to 10% prevalence rate reported in general studies of primary care patients reviewed by Katon and Schulberg (1992). Yeung et al. concluded that their finding of a high prevalence of depression in the primary care setting "adds to the growing evidence that depression is common among Asian and/or Asian-Americans" (p. 28). Using the Center for Epidemiologic Studies-Depression scale (CES-D) to assess nearly 500 Asian Americans, Kuo (1984) reported higher rates of depression in a community sample of Seattle, Washington-area Chinese, Filipino, Japanese, and Korean Americans than among European Americans. In contrast, Takeuchi et al. (1998) analyzed data from the largest national study of Asian Americans, which included more than 2,000 individuals (the National Latino and Asian American Study—NLAAS) and found that Chinese Americans in Los Angeles had a lower lifetime prevalence rate for depression (6.9%) than the national average of 17.1% (Kessler et al., 1994).

Yang and WonPat-Borja's (2006) review of literature on psychopathology among Asian Americans noted that of six community-based studies that focused on Asian American elders, three reported lower rates of depressive symptoms than the general population, two found similar rates, and one found higher rates. Their review also noted one study (Mui, Kang, Chen, & Domanski, 2003) that used a regional probability sample and "found greatly increased rates of positive screens for depression among six elder Asian American groups (average = 40.5%; range = 15%–76%), suggesting that Asian

American elders are at risk for depression" (Yang & WonPat-Borja, p. 396). Within the Mui et al. (2003) study, Japanese American elders had the highest depression scores, followed by Korean American and Filipino American elders. An earlier study by Yamamoto, Rhee, and Chang (1994) found that, compared with a general sample of older adults in St. Louis, Korean American elders living in Los Angeles had a slightly higher lifetime prevalence for dysthymic disorder (2% versus 1.2%) and major depression (1% versus 0.8%).

Generalizations across prevalence rate studies are limited by important differences in sampling, diagnostic criteria and focus, and methodologies. Rather than making broad conclusions about Asian American elders as whole, more recent research suggests the need to focus on specific subgroups and has identified a range of factors that can influence depression prevalence rates, including gender, age of immigration, length of residence in the United States, English proficiency, and refugee status (Hwang, Chun, Takeuchi, Myers, & Siddarth, 2005; Takeuchi et al., 2007). Data from the National Latino and Asian American (NLAAS) study indicated that Asian immigrant women were less likely to have a lifetime prevalence of depression than U.S.-born Asian women. For men in the NLAAS study, lifetime prevalence of depression was associated with English proficiency. Understanding similar complex relationships between gender, acculturative status, and immigration factors is also needed in research on depression rates among APIA elders. For example, Yamamoto et al.'s (1994) previously noted study found an especially high lifetime prevalence of alcohol abuse and dependence among elderly Korean American men. The researchers also noted that Koreans are tolerant of male drinking. If drinking is reflective of a more culturally acceptable response to or expression of depression, then depression prevalence rates may be underestimated for this subgroup of elders. Finally, as noted by Sue, Cheng, Saad, and Chu (2012), it is difficult to determine the accuracy of prevalence data on Asian Americans because of the potential impacts of culturally based reporting biases and cultural biases in how mental disorders are conceptualized.

Additional potential impacts of cognitive decline and isolation for elders can further complicate accurate depression assessment. Although depression is one of the most common psychiatric problems among older adults in general (Fernandez, Levy, Lachar, & Small, 1995) and up to 30% of the elderly population may be struggling with significant depressive symptomatology (Katz, Curil, & Nemetz, 1988), Trinh and Ahmed (2009) noted that two of the largest epidemiologic studies, the Epidemiologic Catchment Area Study (Zhang & Snowden, 1999) and the National Comorbidity Survey (Blazer, Kessler, McGonagle, & Swartz, 1994), were unable to provide accurate estimates of depression among the Asian American elderly. Data on Pacific Islanders is also absent. For example, Held, Nu'usolia, Tuitele, and McGarvey (2010) noted, "No studies have examined depressive symptoms in American Samoa" (p. 462). Hence, data on the prevalence of depression among APIA elders are limited.

Somewhat more data are available on suicide. Reviews by Trinh and Ahmed (2009) and Leong, Leach, Yeh, and Chou (2007) each noted findings that indicated significantly lower overall suicide rates for Asian Americans than those found for European Americans. However, both also point to additional studies that show Asian American elders are at risk for suicide. Baker (1994) analyzed 1990 census data and found that Asian American elders had approximately half the suicide rate of European American elders, but they had the highest rate of completed suicides among ethnic minority groups. Yu, Chang, Liu, and Fernandez (1989) reported that Chinese Americans over the age of 64 and Japanese Americans over the age of 74 had higher rates of suicide than their European American counterparts. Additional results from the Mental Health: Culture, Race, and Ethnicity Supplement to the Surgeon General's Report (U.S. Department of Health and Human Services, 2001) indicated that East Asian women had the highest suicide rate of all women 65 years or older (McKenzie, Serfaty, & Crawford, 2003). Similarly, an examination of completed suicides in the city of San Francisco between 1988 and 1993 revealed that while Caucasian women were at greatest risk to complete suicide between the ages of 45 and 54, Asian women over the age of 85 were at comparatively greater risk to complete suicide by a ratio of 2.7 to 1 (Shiang et al., 1997). Asian men in the same study were at greater risk than Caucasians to complete suicide between the ages of 75 and 84. A 2006 review of literature also noted that older Asian women were at the highest risk for suicide among similar-aged women from all ethnoracial groups (Yang & WonPat-Borja, 2006). Recent data from the Centers for Disease Control and Prevention (CDC) similarly indicate that the risk for suicide among APIA elders is a concern. Among all women age 75 and older who died by suicide, the CDC-reported rate for APIA women was the highest at 8.20 per 100,000. Within the APIA population, however, men age 85 and over have the greatest risk of suicide, with a rate of 23.51 per 100,000 (CDC, 2011; Suicide Prevention Resource Center, 2011). Additional research by Bartels et al. (2002) also found that among the primary care patients over 65 in their study, Asian American elders reported greater levels of death and suicidal ideation than their European American, African American, and Hispanic American peers, although more recent population-based study data indicate that, overall, Asians over the age of 65 were less likely to attempt suicide than other ethnic groups (Cheng et al., 2010). Suicide among American Samoa older adults was found to be rare, with almost all suicides carried out by young men (Rubenstein, 1992); there is typically a second spike in lifespan suicide rates among those over age 65 in most ethnoracial groups, but a similar spike has not been identified for Native Hawaiian and other Pacific Islanders (CDC, 2011; Suicide Prevention Resource Center, 2011).

Risk factors associated with depression in older adults in the general population have been well identified. Specific psychosocial stressors associated with the prevalence of depression in later life include poverty, life events, and lack of companionship (Lin & Ensel, 1984; Ohara, Kohout, & Wallace, 1985; Phifer & Murrel, 1986). Depression in late life also often interacts with medical or neurological illness, which can amplify disability and increase mortality rates (Katz, Streim, & Parmelee, 1994). There is a strong correlation between diabetes and depression in general (Anderson, Freedland, Clouse, & Lustman, 2001), and the high and increasing prevalence of diabetes among Native Hawaiian and American Samoan populations, respectively, have led to investigations of depressive symptoms in this context (e.g., Held et al., 2010; Kaholokula, Haynes, Grandinetti, & Chang, 2006). Although these studies do not focus specifically on older adults, they point to the importance of understanding the potential interrelationships between diabetes and depression among these groups.

Asian American elders are at risk for exposure to the same factors that affect prevalence of depression among the general population but may additionally face discrimination based on their minority status, as mentioned earlier, and additional stressors related to adjustment difficulties associated with immigration. In listing psychosocial predictors of psychological distress among Asian Americans, Uba (1994) cited old age as a factor, in addition to unemployment/low income, being female, social isolation, immigration status, and refugee premigration experience and postmigration adjustment. Hence, an Asian American elder may be more likely to suffer from multiple psychosocial stressors, such as feeling isolated after the death of a spouse or being unemployed/underemployed and sinking into poverty after retirement as a function of being an immigrant and an ethnic minority individual. These additive factors can place them at higher risk for depression and other psychological disorders. There are some data to support this view. Research has found that, compared with younger Southeast Asians, elderly Southeast Asian adults are more at risk for feeling alienated (Nicassio & Pate, 1984) and unhappy (Rumbaut, 1985). Similarly, older Korean Americans were found to be at higher risk for feeling alienated and powerless than younger Korean Americans (Moon & Pearl, 1991).

In addition to the preceding risk factors, immigrant or foreign-born Asian Americans face further stress. Many APIA elders have come to the United States to reunite with their daughters and sons and maintain family ties (Wong & Ujimoto, 1998). These individuals have been equated by Kiefer et al. (1985) to political refugees because these elders would rather have stayed in their home country, but instead they have immigrated to be with their children. Studies have shown that Asian elders who recently immigrated to the United States are at risk for experiencing a loss of cultural identity and status, as well as a lack of support systems. Detzner (1996), for example, noted that some elderly Southeast Asian immigrants associated their loss of an honored position in the family as an abandonment of their identity while living in the United States. Those APIA elders who have immigrated also encounter communication problems, both with more acculturated family members and within the society at large (Cheung, 1989; Kao & Lam, 1997; Kim, Kim, & Hurh, 1991; Tsai & Lopez, 1997).

The effects of immigration are multifold. Each immigrant confronts two sources of stress: the stress of leaving one's native country and the acculturative stress of adapting to a new culture and/or country (Nicassio, Solomon, Guest, & McCullough, 1986). Even though the two are clearly interrelated, it is possible for a person or a group to overcome one stress but not the other. For example, Kim, Hurh, and Kim (1993) reported that older Korean immigrants do not become more Americanized regardless of their length of residence in the United States because they maintain strong social and cultural ethnic attachments. Using qualitative studies, some researchers have attempted to explain the emotional stress of immigration by using a grief model (e.g., Aroian, 1990; Casado & Leung, 2001; Schneller, 1981). Casado and Leung (2001) assessed 150 Chinese immigrants and found that migratory grief, as measured by a questionnaire on how much the participant misses his or her homeland and how much the participant feels isolated in the new country, contributed to 41.5% of the variance in predicting depression. Longing for one's home country and feelings of loneliness appear to be significant risk factors for APIA elders. From an assessment perspective, clinicians should explore the possibility of migratory grief and the related question of how much the client misses the homeland, as well as the frequency of contacts with and visits to the homeland. Explorations of immigration stressors and migratory grief among APIA elders are especially critical because depression and higher rates of suicide have been found to be greater among elderly Chinese immigrants than for U.S.-born Chinese Americans (Yu et al., 1989).

Treatment Issues

Before addressing strategies for treating depression in Asian American elders, it is helpful to understand the challenges related to doing so. These challenges can affect the assessment of depression itself as well as intervention efforts. There are specific barriers within each of these challenges, but often the barriers overlap. General challenges that apply to both assessment and treatment of depression include understandings of mental illnesses and therapy, language barriers, and financial and transportation barriers. Consider the following brief vignette.

> A 67-year-old Chinese widow has been referred by a primary care physician stating that she "feels unwell." She reports difficulty falling and staying asleep, feeling agitated, and has experienced stomach upsets and weight loss that cannot be attributed to a medical illness.

From a traditional Western perspective, where mental problems have typically been considered separate from physical problems, it might seem surprising that the client in the vignette has been referred by her primary care physician. However, psychological referrals of older adults across ethnic groups often come from medical care providers, with whom they have the most frequent contact (La Rue & Watson, 1998). In addition, Asian cultures view the mind and body in harmony, and Asian American elders are much more likely to

present their distress to a physician than to a mental health professional. Chinese elders do not tend to report mental health problems,
and headaches, back pain, or other psychosomatic complaints are
more common expressions of distress than emotional complaints
(Casado & Leung, 2001). Therefore, seeking care from a physician
is much more likely than seeking help from a mental health professional. The emphasis on somatic complaints also has implications for
treatment. Weisman et al. (2005) suggest the importance of allow-
ing Asian American elders ample time to first express their physical concerns. Once this has been encouraged, clients may feel more
comfortable raising emotional issues. Weisman et al. (2005) also
note that the incorporation of somatic psychological treatments can
work well with the presentation of somatic complaints among Asian
clients. Progressive relaxation, mindful meditation, or deep muscle
relaxation are all techniques that may be useful for the client in the
vignette to the degree that there is agitation and/or anxiety related
to depressive symptoms. These techniques may be helpful in that
they are consistent with a cultural focus on somatic distress and can
lead to the experience of somatic relief through reduced body tension. Flaskerud and Hu (1992) have also suggested that psychotropic
medications may be effective with APIA clients for the treatment of
depression because such medications are in line with the tendency
to somaticize symptoms, although it would clearly be important to
assess the overall health concerns of elders when considering such
medical interventions.

Culture also plays a role in shaping the ways in which APIA elders
cope with mental distress. Wong and Ujimoto (1998) indicate that
culture can (a) influence a person's understanding of what is stress-
ful, (b) determine how a person reacts to stress, (c) dictate the use
of resources, (d) impact understanding of what coping behavior is
appropriate, and (e) influence expression of coping outcomes. For
many APIA elders, the concept of psychotherapy is foreign and even
unacceptable. Because many Asian Americans and immigrants associate shame and stigma with mental illness (Kinzie & Mason, 1983),

they are more likely to seek help through friends, family, and/or religious leaders (Moon & Tashima, 1982; Nishio & Bilmes, 1987). This suggests the importance of recognizing that referrals are likely to come through non-mental-health channels (as described in the vignette).

It is also critical to assess the elder client's level of English proficiency, which has relevance to the assessment of depressive symptoms as well as treatment. Kuo and Tsai (1986, as cited in Lam et al., 1997) reported that problems with the English language are the most common difficulty among Asian American immigrants. Based on the U.S. Census Bureau's 2009 American Community Survey, most Asians (77% of those above age 5) spoke a language other than English at home (Johnson, Ríos, Drewery, Ennis, & Kim, 2010). The proportion ranged from 46% for Japanese to 89% for Vietnamese. Fifty percent of those APIA in the 2007 American Community Survey who spoke a language other than English reported that they spoke English less than "very well" (Shin & Kominski, 2010). These data are important because research has demonstrated that poor English proficiency is related to depressive symptoms among Chinese Americans (Casado & Leung, 2001; Lam et al., 1997), Korean Americans (Hyun, 2001), and Southeast Asian refugees (Nicassio et al., 1986). Because the lack of English proficiency has significant implications for all levels of evaluation in terms of referral, assessment, and treatment, it may be just as important to have bilingual speakers or interpreters for the initial phone call or assessment phase as it is to have language assistance during the actual treatment.

The clinical vignette is noteworthy for the presentation of somatic symptoms, as well as for the absence of symptoms related to affect. However, Asian cultural values, in addition to language difficulties, can influence the self-report of depressive emotions. For example, Japanese American elders may adhere to value of *gaman*, which in traditional Japanese culture refers to self-control or a tendency to suppress emotions, whether positive or negative (Kobata, 1979). Whereas Ujimoto, Nishio, Wong, and Lam (1992) identified this tendency as an important factor to successful aging as reported by Japanese elders, Tomita (1994) pointed out that it may also prevent the identification of victims of elder abuse. The suppression of emotions, which has also been observed in Chinese immigrants (Mui, 1996), may also lead APIA elders to minimize or refrain from expressions of distress associated with depression, making detection of depression especially difficult. Pang (1995), who conducted a study with more than 600 elderly Korean immigrants, suggests that it may be more useful to assess depressive symptoms by asking about loneliness rather than by asking about depressive feeling or emotions because an open admission of depression is culturally stigmatized and acknowledgment of loneliness is less problematic.

Economic resources must also be considered in addressing treatments for APIA elders. Many who are recent immigrants, especially those who are refugees, may be unemployed, self-employed, or in low-paying jobs with minimal benefits. As a result, they are less likely to have adequate health insurance that might facilitate mental health care options. Furthermore, the Personal Responsibility and Work Opportunity Reconciliation Act of 1996 (PRWORA) prohibits certain immigrants who entered the United States on or after August 22, 1996, from receiving Medicaid or State Children's Health Insurance Program (SCHIP) benefits for 5 years. Many private insurance policies will not add an elderly parent to the family plan of an adult child. Such economic challenges, coupled with language barriers and cultural inhibitions to seeking mental health services, add further to the difficulties in treating elder APIA depression. Some researchers suggest that a critical response to assist older Asians is to help them obtain citizenship as well as social security (Havemann, 1997; Jacobs, 1997). This type of advocacy would enhance access to services for APIA elders through a broader level of system intervention.

Cultural transition and migration are among the greatest challenges for Asian elders. In traditional Asian culture, filial piety and respect for the elderly are two Confucian ideals with a long historical legacy in East Asia extending from China across Korea and Japan and into Vietnam. For the Chinese, old age has traditionally been a symbol of status (Cheung, Cho, Lum, Tang, & Yau, 1980; Ikels, 1983). Filial piety represents the obligations, respect, and duty that a person has to his or her parents. Allegiance to parents is primary and expected from male children, even after they have married and begun a family of their own (Lee, 1997). These APIA elders are often seen as doing well because outsiders assume that they benefit from the extensive family support that has traditionally characterized their cultures. However, even though Asian American elders are more likely to be cared for by their children than other ethnic groups' elders are, the frequency of such filial piety is shifting and cannot be assumed to exist. Kim, Kim, and Hurh (1991) found that Korean immigrants may find it difficult to carry out filial piety in the United States, and Lan (2002, as cited in Wong, Yoo, & Stewart, 2006) notes that older Chinese and Korean parents living in the United States are more likely to live separately from their adult children. Although many APIA elders immigrated to the United States to be with their children (Koh & Bell, 1987), they may find themselves living alone and greatly disappointed. Therefore, in considering the clinical vignette, it is important to determine whether the client is living alone, particularly because living alone has been found to be a significant predictor of depression among both Chinese (Mui, 1996) and Korean (Mui, 2001) immigrants. Because Chinese American older women have a higher risk for suicide, one also needs to consider gender, in combination with living alone, in assessing the severity of distress for the client presented in the vignette.

Although the loss of family role status and intergenerational family stressors can have serious mental health consequences for APIA elders, the family can also be an important source of support. The enlistment of family can be instrumental in treatment. Ho (1987) notes that Asians and Pacific Islanders strongly value family, and what family members think of them carries great significance. As a result, a family member may be instrumental in encouraging an elder to seek services or to participate in treatment. Fujii, Fukushima, and Yamamoto (1993), for example, describe a case example of a severely depressed Japanese American elder who initially refused antidepressant medications but later agreed to take the medications after family members urged him to do so.

If depression of the elder is related to intergenerational tensions and the family is willing to participate in therapy together, the "bicultural effectiveness training" (BET) developed by Szapocznik and Kurtines (1993) may be an effective strategy that addresses the family system rather than the elder in isolation. Weisman et al. (2005) note that BET can help in "reframing cultural conflict as the 'identified patient' to which the family's 'ailment' can be attributed" (p. 647). For APIA elders who live alone and for whom family therapy is not possible, treatment should include efforts to identify friendship or community support networks (Mui, 1996, 2001). These networks can provide the elder with a place to express dissatisfaction with their children and reduce feelings of alienation and isolation.

Often APIA elders turn to traditional forms of healing that should also be recognized when formulating treatment plans. More than 80% of immigrant Cambodian elders living in California reported using traditional South Asian treatments for their emotional and physical problems (Handelman & Yeo, 1996, as cited in Weisman et al., 2005). For Chinese elders, traditional healing might include herbal medicines and acupuncture. Korean elders may visit *hanui* (practitioners of traditional Korean medicine). Given the prevalence of traditional healing practices, the combination of Western and traditional Asian healing practices can be especially effective (Sakauye, 1992).

Issues of power and authority must be carefully considered when implementing any of the treatment approaches with APIA elders that have been described. As previously discussed, there is evidence that Asian Americans may be especially reliant on authoritative aspects of the psychotherapeutic relationship (Chin, 1998), which may lead them to assume a deferential communication pattern (Matsui,

1996) so as not to appear burdensome. At the same time, however, clinicians must be mindful of the need to communicate respect for the role and authority of the elder. One way to communicate this respect is to elicit frequent feedback from the client (Weisman et al., 2005).

Summary

Although APIA elders have been underrepresented in mental health services, they can experience significant levels of distress. The assessment and treatment of depression within this group require attention to multiple concerns, including the wide range of ethnicities, immigration histories, and acculturation backgrounds among APIA; the importance of language, cultural beliefs that can influence help seeking, symptom presentation, and treatment options; and the impact of traditional roles and intergenerational stresses for immigrant elders.

Note

1. On February 19, 1942, shortly after the Japanese military attacked Pearl Harbor, President Franklin D. Roosevelt signed Executive Order 9066, which allowed military commanders to remove more than 110,000 Japanese Americans from their homes along western portions of the U.S. mainland and confine them in isolated incarceration camps. The American government portrayed the removal as a military necessity to protect against potential acts of sabotage or disloyalty by any individual of Japanese heritage. Denied the right to a trial or individual review, the affected Japanese Americans, 62% of whom were U.S. citizens, were confined to the camps for an average of 2 to 3 years. In the early 1980s, the Commission on Wartime Relocation and Internment of Civilians (CWRIC) conducted a full review of the circumstances surrounding the government's actions. The commission concluded that the executive order was not justified by military

necessity and that the incarceration was instead shaped by "race prejudice, war hysteria and a failure of political leadership" (Commission on Wartime Relocation and Internment of Civilians, 1982, p. 5). In 1988, Congress passed and President Ronald Reagan signed the Civil Liberties Act, which provided a formal apology and a single payment of $20,000 for each surviving internee. The terminology referring to the Japanese American camps has changed over time (see Densho website). Though they are often referred to as internment camps, scholars note that the term *internment camp* refers to specific camps that held enemy aliens and were separate from the 10 main camps where the majority of Japanese Americans were held. For this reason, many now consider the term *incarceration camp* or *concentration camp* to be more accurate.

References

Administration on Aging. (2012). *A profile of older Americans: 2012.* Retrieved from http://www.aoa.gov/Aging_Statistics/Profile/2012/docs/2012profile.pdf

Aldwin, C., & Greenberger, E. (1987). Cultural differences in the predictors of depression. *American Journal of Community Psychology,* 15, 789–813.

Anderson, R., Freedland, K., Clouse, R. E., & Lustman, P. J. (2001). The prevalence of comorbid depression in adults with diabetes: A metaanalysis. *Diabetes Care, 24,* 1069–1078.

Aroian, K. L. (1990). A model of psychological adaptation to migration and resettlement. *Nursing Research, 39,* 5–10.

Baker, F. M. (1994). Suicide among ethnic minority elderly: A statistical and psychosocial perspective. *Journal of Geriatric Psychiatry, 27,* 241–264.

Bartels, S. J., Coakley, E., Oxman, T. E., Constantino, G., Oslin, D., Chen, H., & Sanchez, H. (2002). Suicidal ideation in older primary care patients with depression, anxiety, and at-risk alcohol use. *American Journal of Geriatric Psychiatry, 10,* 417–427.

Blazer, D. G., Kessler, R. C., McGonagle, K. A., & Swartz, M. S. (1994). The prevalence and distribution of major depression in a national community sample: The National Comorbidity Survey. *American Journal of Psychiatry, 151,* 979–986.

Browne, C., Fong, R., & Mokuau, N. (1994). The mental health of Asian and Pacific Island elders: Implications for research and mental health administration. *Journal of Mental Health Administration*, 21(1), 52–60.

Casado, B. L., & Leung, P. (2001). Migratory grief and depression among elderly Chinese American immigrants. *Social Work Practice with the Asian American Elderly*, 36(1–2), 5–26.

Centers for Disease Control and Prevention (CDC). (2011). *Web-based Injury Statistics Query and Reporting System (WISQARS)*. Retrieved from http://www.cdc.gov/ncipc/wisqars

Cheng, J. K. Y., Fancher, T. L., Ratanasen, M., Conner, K. R., Duberstein, P. R., Sue, S., & Takeuchi, D. (2010). Lifetime suicidal ideation and suicide attempts in Asian Americans. *Asian American Journal of Psychology*, 1, 18–30.

Cheung, L. Y. S., Cho, E. R., Lum, D., Tang, T. Y., & Yau, H. B. (1980). The Chinese elderly and family structure: Implications for health care. *Public Health Reports*, 95(5), 491–495.

Cheung, M. (1989). Elderly Chinese living in the United States. *Social Work*, 34, 457–461.

Chin, J. L. (1998). *Mental health services and treatment*. Thousand Oaks, CA: Sage.

Commission on Wartime Relocation and Internment of Civilians. (1982). *Personal justice denied: Report of the commission on wartime relocation and internment of civilians: Part 2, Recommendations*. Washington, DC: U.S. Government Printing Office.

Densho: The Japanese American legacy project. Retrieved from http://www.densho.org/default.asp?path=/assets/sharedpages/glossary.asp?section=home

Detzner, D. F. (1996). No place without a home: Southeast Asian grandparents in refugee families. *Generations*, 20(1), 45–48.

Fernandez, F., Levy, J. K., Lachar, B. L., & Small, G. W. (1995). The management of depression and anxiety in the elderly. *Journal of Clinical Psychiatry*, 56(2), 20–29.

Flaskerud, J. H., & Hu, L. T. (1992). Relationship of ethnicity to psychiatric diagnosis. *Journal of Nervous and Mental Disease*, 180, 296–303.

Fujii, J. S., Fukushima, S. N., & Yamamoto, J. (1993). Psychiatric care of Japanese Americans. In A. C. Gaw (Ed.), *Culture, ethnicity, and mental illness* (pp. 305–345). Washington, DC: American Psychiatric Press.

Grieco, E. M., Acosta, Y. D., de la Cruz, G. P., Gambino, C., Gryn, T., Larsen, L. J.,...Walters, N. P. (2012). *The foreign-born population in the United States: 2010.* Retrieved from http://www.census.gov/prod/2012pubs/acs-19.pdf

Handelman, L., & Yeo, G. (1996). Using explanatory models to understand chronic symptoms of Cambodian refugees. *Family Medicine, 28,* 271–276.

Havemann, J. (1997, March 27). Suit challenges welfare law. Immigrant cutoffs called unlawful. *Globe,* p. A3.

Held, R. F., Nu'usolia, O., Tuitele, J., & McGarvey, S. (2010). Patient and health care provider views of depressive symptoms in American Samoa. *Cultural Diversity and Ethnic Minority Psychology, 16,* 461–467.

Hixson, L., Hepler, B. B., & Kim, M. O. (2012). *The Native Hawaiian and other Pacific Islander Population: 2010.* Retrieved from http://www.census.gov/prod/cen2010/briefs/c2010br-12.pdf

Ho, M. K. (1987). *Family therapy with ethnic minorities.* Newbury Park, CA: Sage.

Hoeffel, E. M., Rastogi, S., Kim, M. O., & Shahid, H. *The Asian population: 2010.* Retrieved from http://www.census.gov/prod/cen2010/briefs/c2010br-11.pdf

Hwang, W. C., Chun, C. A., Takeuchi, D. T., Myers, H. F., & Siddarth, P. (2005) Age of first onset major depression in Chinese Americans. *Cultural Diversity and Ethnic Minority Psychology, 11,* 16–27.

Hymes, R. W., & Akiyama, M. (1991). Depression and self-enhancement among Japanese and American students. *Journal of Social Psychology, 131,* 321–334.

Hyun, K. J. (2001). Is an independent self a requisite for Asian immigrants' psychological well-being in the U.S.? The case of Korean Americans. *Journal of Human Behavior in the Social Environment, 3*(3–4), 179–200.

Ikels, C. (1983). *Aging and adaptation: Chinese in Hong Kong and the United States.* Hamden, CT: Archon Books.

Iwamasa, G. Y., & Hilliard, K. M. (1999). Depression and anxiety among Asian American elders: A review of the literature. *Clinical Psychology Review, 19*(3), 343–357.

Iwamasa, G. Y., & Sorocco, K. H. (2007). The psychology of Asian American older adults. In F. T. L. Leong, A. G. Inman, A. Ebreo, L. H. Yang, L. Kinoshita, & M. Fu (Eds.), *Handbook of Asian American psychology* (2nd ed., pp. 213–226). Thousand Oaks, CA: Sage.

Jacobs, S. (1997, March 16). Immigrants face test of lifetime: Amid benefit cuts, noncitizens are scrambling for answers. *Globe*, pp. A1, A30.

Johnson, T. D., Rios, M., Drewery, M. P., Ennis, S. R., & Kim, M. O. (2010). *People who spoke a language other than English at home by Hispanic origin and race: 2009 American community survey briefs.* Washington, DC: U.S. Census Bureau.

Kaholokula, J. K., Haynes, S. N., Grandinetti, A., & Chang, H. K. (2006). Ethnic differences in the relationship between depressive symptoms and Health-Related Quality of Life with people with type 2 diabetes. *Ethnicity and Health, 11,* 59–80.

Kao, S.-K. R., & Lam, M. L. (1997). Asian American elderly. In E. Lee (Ed.), *Working with Asian Americans: A guide for clinicians* (pp. 122–139). New York, NY: Guilford Press.

Katon, W., & Schulberg, H. (1992). Epidemiology of depression in primary care. *General Hospital Psychiatry,14,* 237–247.

Katz, I. R., Curil, S., & Nemetz, A. (1988). Functional psychiatric disorders in the elderly. In L. W. Lazarus (Ed.), *Essentials of geriatric psychiatry* (pp. 113–137). New York, NY: Springer.

Katz, I. R., Streim, J., & Parmelee, P. (1994). Prevention of depression, recurrences, and complications in later life. *Preventive Medicine: An International Journal Devoted to Practice and Theory, 23*(5), 734–750.

Kessler, R. C., McGonagle, K. A., Zhao, S., Nelson, C.B., Hughes, M., Eshleman, S., & Kendler, K. S. (1994). Lifetime and 12-month prevalence of DSM-III-R psychiatric disorders in the United States: Results from the National Comorbidity Survey. *Archives of General Psychiatry, 51,* 8–19.

Kiefer, C. W., Kim, S., Choi, K., Kim, L., Kim, B., Shon, S., & Kim, T. (1985). Adjustment problems of Korean American elderly. *The Gerontologist, 25,* 477–482.

Kim, K. C., Hurh, W. M., & Kim, S. (1993). Generation differences in Korean immigrants' life conditions in the United States. *Sociological Perspectives, 36*(3), 257–270.

Kim, K. C., Kim, S., & Hurh, W. M. (1991). Filial piety and intergenerational relationship in Korean immigrant families. *Intergenerational Journal of Aging and Human Development, 33,* 233–245.

Kinzie, J. D., & Mason, S. (1983). Five years' experience with Indochinese refugee psychiatric patients. *Journal of Operational Psychiatry, 14*(2), 105–111.

Kitano, H. H. L., & Daniels, R. (1995). *Asian Americans: Emerging minorities* (2nd ed.). Englewood Cliffs, NJ: Prentice Hall.

Kobata, F. (1979). The influence of culture on family relations: The Asian American experience. In P. Ragan (Ed.), *Aging parents* (pp. 94–106). Los Angeles, CA: University of Southern California Press.

Koh, J. Y., & Bell, W. G. (1987). Korean elders in the United States: Intergenerational relations and living arrangements. *The Gerontologist, 27,* 66–71.

Kuo, W. H. (1984). Prevalence of depression among Asian Americans. *Journal of Nervous and Mental Disease, 172,* 449–457.

Kuo, W. H., & Tsai, Y. M. (1986). Social networking, hardiness, and immigrants' mental health. *Journal of Health and Social Behavior, 27,* 133–149.

La Rue, A., & Watson, J. (1998). Psychological assessment of older adults. *Professional Psychology: Research and Practice, 295,* 5–14.

Lam, R. D., Pacala, J. T., & Smith, S. L. (1997). Factors related to depressive symptoms in an elderly Chinese American sample. *Clinical Gerontologist, 17*(4), 57–70.

Lan, P. C. (2002). Subcontracting filial piety. *Journal of Family Issues, 23,* 812–835.

Lee, E. (1997). *Working with Asian Americans: A guide for clinicians.* New York, NY: Guilford Press.

Leong, F. T. L., Leach, M. M., Yeh, C., & Chou, E. (2007). Suicide among Asian Americans: What do we know? What do we need to know? *Death Studies, 31,* 417–434.

Lin, N., & Ensel, W. M. (1984). Depression mobility and its social etiology: The role of life events and social support. *Journal of Health and Social Behavior, 25,* 176–188.

Matsui, W. T. (1996). Japanese American families. In M. McGoldrick, J. Giordano, & J. K. Pearce (Eds.), *Ethnicity and family therapy* (pp. 268–280). New York, NY: Guilford Press.

McKenzie, K., Serfaty, M., & Crawford, M. (2003). Suicide in ethnic minority groups. *British Journal of Psychiatry, 183,* 100–101.

Moon, A., & Tashima, N. (1982). *Help seeking behavior and attitudes of Southeast Asian refugees.* San Francisco, CA: Pacific Asian Mental Health Research Project.

Moon, J., & Pearl, J. (1991). Alienation of elderly Korean American immigrants as related to place of residence, gender, age, years of education, time in the US, living with or without children, and living with or without a spouse. *International Journal of Aging and Human Development, 32,* 115–124.

Mui, A. C. (1996). Depression among elderly Chinese immigrants: An explanatory study. *Social Work, 41,* 633–645.

Mui, A. C. (2001). Stress, coping, and depression among elderly Korean immigrants. *Journal of Human Behavior in the Social Environment, 3,* 281–299.

Mui, A. C., Kang, S. Y., Chen, L. M., & Domanski, M. D. (2003). Reliability of the Geriatric Depression Scale for use among elderly Korean immigrants in the USA. *International Psychgeriatrics, 15,* 253–271.

Nagata, D. K. (1998). Intergenerational effects of the Japanese American internment. In Y. Danieli (Ed.), *International handbook of multigenerational legacies of trauma* (pp. 433–456). New York, NY: Plenum.

Nicassio, P. M., & Pate, J. K. (1984). An analysis of problems of resettlement of the Indochinese refugees in the United States. *Social Psychiatry, 19*(3), 135–141.

Nicassio, P. M., Solomon, G. S., Guest, S. S., & McCullough, J. E. (1986). Emigration stress and language proficiency as correlates of depression in a sample of Southeast Asian refugees. *International Journal of Social Psychiatry, 32,* 22–28.

Nishio, H. K., & Bilmes, M. (1987). Psychotherapy with Southeast Asian American clients. *Professional Psychology: Research and Practice, 18,* 1029–1036.

Ohara, M. W., Kohout, F. J., & Wallace, R. B. (1985). Depression among the rural elderly. *Journal of Nervous and Mental Disease, 173,* 582–589.

Pang, K. Y. (1995). A cross-cultural understanding of depression among elderly Korean immigrants: Prevalence, symptoms, and diagnosis. *Clinical Gerontology, 15,* 3–20.

Phifer, J. F., & Murrel, S. A. (1986). Etiologic factors in the onset of depressive symptoms in older adults. *Journal of Abnormal Psychology, 95,* 282–291.

Rubenstein, D. H. (1992). Suicide in Micronesia and Samoa: A critical review of explanations. *Pacific Studies, 15,* 51–75.

Rumbaut, R. G. (1985). Mental health and the refugee experience: A comparative study of Southeast Asian refugees. In T. C. Owan (Ed.),

Southeast Asian mental health: Treatment, prevention, services, train-ing, and research (pp. 433–486). Washington, DC: National Institute of Mental Health.

Sakauye, K. (1992). The elderly Asian patient. *Journal of Geriatric Psychiatry, 25*, 85–104.

Schneller, D. (1981). The immigrant's challenge: Mourning the loss of homeland and adapting to the new world. *Smith College Studies in Social Work, 51*(2), 95–125.

Shiang, J., Blinn, R., Bongar, B., Stephens, B., Allison, D., & Schatzberg, A. (1997). Suicide in San Francisco, CA: A compari-son of Caucasian and Asian groups, 1987–1994. *Suicide and Life Threatening Behavior, 27*, 80–91.

Shin, H. B., & Kominski, R. A. (2010). *Language use in the United States: 2007.* Retrieved from http://www.census.gov/hhes/socdemo/language/data/acs/ACS-12.pdf

Sue, S. (1991). Ethnicity and culture in psychological research and prac-tice. In J. D. Goodchilds (Ed.), *Psychological perspectives on human diversity in America* (pp. 51–85). Washington, DC: American Psychological Association.

Sue, S., Cheng, J. K. Y., Saad, C. S., & Chu, J. (2012). Asian American mental health: A call to action. *American Psychologist, 67*, 532–544.

Suicide Prevention Resource Center. (2011). *Suicide among racial/ethnic populations in the U.S.: Asians, Pacific Islanders, and Native Hawaiians.* Newton, MA: Education Development Center, Inc.

Szapocznik, J., & Kurtines, W. M. (1993). Family psychology and cul-tural diversity: Opportunities for theory, research, and applica-tion. *American Psychologist, 48*, 400–407.

Takaki, R. (1989). *Strangers from a different shore: A history of Asian Americans.* Boston, MA: Little, Brown.

Takeuchi, D. T., Chung, R. C. Y., Lin, K. M., Shen, H., Kurasaki, K., Chun, C. A., & Sue, S. (1998). Lifetime and twelve-month prev-alence rates of major depressive episodes and dysthmia among Chinese Americans in Los Angeles. *American Journal of Psychiatry, 155*, 1407–1414.

Takeuchi, D. T., Zane, N., Hong, S., Chae, D. H., Gong, F., Gee, G. C.,…Alegría, M. (2007). Immigration- related factors and mental disorders among Asian Americans. *American Journal of Public Health, 97*, 84–90.

Toarmino, D., & Chun, C. (1997). Issues and strategies in counseling Korean Americans. In C. C. Lee (Ed.), *Multicultural issues in counseling: New approaches to diversity* (2nd ed., pp. 233–254). Alexandria, VA: American Counseling Association.

Tomita, S. K. (1994). Consideration of cultural factors in the research of elder mistreatment with an in-depth look at the Japanese. *Journal of Cross-Cultural Gerontology, 9*(1), 39–52.

Trinh, N.-H., & Ahmed, I. (2009). Acculturation and Asian American elderly. In J. F. Rosenbaum, N.-H. Trinh, Y. C. Rho, F. G. Lu, & K. M. Sanders (Eds.), *Handbook of mental health and acculturation in Asian American families* (pp. 167–178). Totowa, NJ: Humana Press.

True, R. H., & Guillermo, T. (1996). Asian/Pacific Islander American women. In M. Bayne-Smith (Ed.), *Race, gender, and health* (pp. 94–120). Thousand Oaks, CA: Sage.

Tsai, D. T., & Lopez, R. A. (1997). The use of social supports by elderly Chinese immigrants. *Journal of Gerontological Social Work, 29*, 77–94.

Uba, L. (1994). *Asian Americans: Personality patterns, identity, and mental health.* New York, NY: Guilford Press.

Ujimoto, K. V., Nishio, H. K., Wong, P. T. P., & Lam, L. (1992). Cultural factors affecting the self-assessment of health satisfaction. In R. Masi, L. Mensah, & K. McLeod (Eds.), *Health and cultures: Explaining the relationships* (pp. 229–240). Toronto, Canada: Canadian Council on Multicultural Health.

U.S. Department of Health and Human Services. (2001). *Mental health: Culture, race and ethnicity–A supplement to Mental health: A report of the Surgeon General.* Rockville, MD: U.S. Department of Health and Human Services, Substance Abuse and Mental Health Services Administration, Center for Mental Health Services.

Weisman, A., Feldman, G., Gruman, C., Rosenberg, R., Chamoro, R., & Belozersky, I. (2005). Improving mental health services for Latino and Asian immigrant elders. *Professional Psychology: Research and Practice, 36*, 642–648.

Werner, C. A. (2011). *The older population: 2010.* Retrieved from http://www.census.gov/prod/cen2010/briefs/c2010br-09.pdf

Wong, P. T. P., & Ujimoto, K. V. (1998). The elderly: Their stress, coping, and mental health. In L. C. Lee & N. W. S. Zane (Eds.), *Handbook of Asian American psychology* (pp. 165–209). Thousand Oaks, CA: Sage.

Wong, S. T., Yoo, G. J., & Stewart, A. L. (2006). The changing meaning of family support among older Chinese and Korean immigrants. *Journal of Gerontology, 61B*, S4–S9.

Wykle, M. L., & Ford, A. B. (1999). *Serving minority elders in the 21st century.* New York, NY: Springer.

Yamamoto, J., Rhee, S., & Chang, D. (1994). Psychiatric disorders among elderly Koreans in the United States. *Community Mental Health Journal, 30,* 17–27.

Yang, L. H., & WonPat-Borja, A. J. (2006). Psychopathology among Asian Americans. In F. T. L. Leong, A. G. Inman, A. Ebreo, L. H. Yang, L. Kinoshita, & M. Fu (Eds.), *Handbook of Asian American psychology* (2nd ed., pp. 379–405). Thousand Oaks, CA: Sage.

Yeung, A., Chan, R., Mischoulon, D., Sonawalla, A., Wong, E., Nierenberg, A. A., & Fava, M. (2004). Prevalence of major depressive disorder among Chinese Americans in primary care. *General Hospital Psychiatry, 26,* 24–30.

Ying, Y. W. (1988). Depressive symptomatology among Chinese-Americans as measured by the CES-D. *Journal of Clinical Psychology, 44,* 734–746.

Young, K., & Takeuchi, D. T. (1998). Racism. In L. C. Lee & N. W. S. Zane (Eds.), *Handbook of Asian American psychology* (pp. 401–432). Thousand Oaks, CA: Sage.

Yu, E., Chang, C. F., Liu, W., & Fernandez, M. (1989). Suicide among Asian American youth. In M. Feinleib (Ed.), *Report of the secretary's task force on youth suicide* (pp. 157–176). Washington, DC: U.S. Department of Health and Human Services.

Zane, N., Morton, T., Chu, J., & Lin, N. (2004). Counseling and psychotherapy with Asian American clients. In T. B. Smith (Ed.), *Practicing multiculturalism: Affirming diversity in counseling and psychology.* Boston, MA: Allyn and Bacon.

Zhang, A. Y., & Snowden, L. R. (1999). Ethnic characteristics of mental disorders in five US communities. *Cultural Diversity and Ethnic Minority Psychology, 5,* 134–146.

4

Psychodynamic Treatment of an Asian American Male with Dual Diagnosis

SONI KIM

Mental Health Treatment of Asian Americans

Most of the existing studies that examine mental health services utilization of Asian Americans show consistently that Asian Americans underutilize mental health services (Lin, 1994; Sue, 1977; U.S. Department of Health and Human Services, 2001). Most authors of these studies attribute this underutilization to a lack of fit between Western understanding of the origins and treatment of psychopathology and Asian values (e.g., Lee & Zane, 1998; Uba, 1994) and recommend that the mental health community consider relevant aspects of Asian culture when providing mental health services to Asian Americans.

One of the more frequent recommendations in psychological literature is to provide a directive style of counseling to Asian Americans rather than an affectively based nondirective approach (Atkinson, Maruyama, & Matsui, 1978; Atkinson & Matushita, 1991; Leong, 1986). However, the majority of the studies that recommend a logical, directive style of counseling base their recommendations on the findings from either audiovisual analogue designs (participants are shown a video of different approaches of counseling and are asked to rate their perception of effectiveness and/or likelihood of seeking such services) or ratings based on attending a single session in a non-clinical setting (research participants attend a single session and are asked to rate their feelings and reactions to the session).

Although such generalizations are typically made, it could be argued that the extent to which the findings from experimental settings apply to organic psychotherapeutic relationships for Asian American population is unknown, and it would stand to reason that a good therapy fit depends on many factors, only one of which is the client's initial perception of effectiveness. Other studies have failed to replicate the finding that Asian Americans prefer a logical, directive counseling style (Atkinson, Poston, Furlong, & Mercado, 1989; Lee & Mixon, 1995; Wong, Kim, Zane, Kim, & Huang, 2003), suggesting that there are many salient variables that determine counseling style preferences of Asian Americans and that factors that have been found to be effective in psychotherapy relationships overall, such as a therapist's empathy toward a client and the strength of therapeutic alliance, apply to Asian Americans as well. There is an emerging literature that discusses alternative approaches to culturally responsive psychotherapy, such as *Race, Culture, and Psychotherapy* (Moodley & Palmer, 2006), which discusses culturally relevant psychotherapy factors within the psychoanalytic framework. This chapter discusses a course of psychotherapy with an Asian American man that utilized a psychodynamic framework.

Defining Psychodynamic Concepts Utilized in Treatment

The approach used to treat the client in this chapter can be described broadly as psychodynamic. Just as the term *psychoanalysis* can describe a wide range of treatment approaches (i.e., "classical Freudian" to "contemporary" intersubjectivity; see Stolorow, Atwood, & Orange, 2002, for descriptions of contemporary thoughts in psychoanalysis), the term *psychodynamic therapy* can encompass approaches described by a wide range of authors. Generally, psychodynamic therapy is insight-oriented and views psychopathology as arising from largely unconscious psychodynamic conflicts that likely began in childhood. To manage inner conflicts that seem irresolvable, people develop ways to cope with those situations that perpetuate, even when the original conflicts are no longer present. For example, a child who perceives a parent to be fragile may learn to cope with the fear of losing the parent by becoming overly competent or controlling. Even after the child becomes an adult and no longer depends on the parent, he may not be able to be sufficiently vulnerable to receive, or tolerate, help or support, leading to possible isolation and/or burnout.

Because the ways of coping often become second nature (become unconscious), they are difficult to become aware of (make conscious), and the role of a psychodynamic psychotherapist is to provide a safe environment for the client to engage in the work to understand and change the dynamics that cause distress. The therapist attends to the information presented in the session (the client's verbal reports as well as the relationship that unfolds in the therapy room) to identify patterns that may be contributing to the client's difficulties and help the client understand the origin and function of the behavior ("insight") so that the patterns the client had assumed were defining parts of him become optional and, therefore, changeable.

Various psychoanalytic theories articulate what unconscious patterns to look for and provide the framework within which to understand the development of these patterns and to understand what techniques can help the client engage in new behaviors. For example, within the self psychology framework as articulated by Heinz Kohut (Siegel, 1996), a person who is driven to seek praise and admiration above all else and at all costs likely suffers from deep depression and a fractured sense of self and likely did not have sufficient opportunities to form a cohesive sense of self as a desirable, lovable being during her formative years. To treat such conditions, the therapist engages in active mirroring, which is a process of reflecting to the client a lovable self; provides empathy to increase the client's self-acceptance; and engages in a consistently positive relationship within the therapeutic boundaries to provide emotionally corrective experiences. Mirroring helps the client feel safer in relationships without the constant need to prove herself (see Greenberg & Mitchell, 1983 for an overview of various psychoanalytic theories).

Asian Americans and Substance Use

Although Asian Americans as a group are reported to experience lower rates of overall substance and illegal drug use than the American population as a whole (2.7% vs. 6.3%, as reported in *Drug Use Among Racial/Ethnic Minorities*, 2003), the rates of substance use among Asian American ethnicities vary. For example, the rate of Korean Americans' illegal drug use (6.7%) surpasses that of the overall U.S. population, and Japanese Americans' usage nears that of the general population (5%). Although no specific reasons for these differences were identified in the report, there are indications that the rates of mental health problems and substance use vary among different Asian countries (Fugita & Crittenden, 1990; Kim, 1998; Kim & Chun, 1993; Kuo, 1984), suggesting that the different mental health and substance abuse rates among Asian Americans may be, in part, a reflection of the problems in the countries of origin.

Each group's immigration history to the United States may also play a role because the reasons for immigration and recency of immigration can affect the overall distress level. Given these factors, it is helpful to have some knowledge of a client's country of origin and the immigration history of the group and the individual when working with Asian Americans so that the therapist can have a more complete understanding of the context of the client's presenting problems.

When working with clients who present with both a history of substance abuse and psychiatric symptoms, it is important to assess thoroughly so that proper treatment can be provided. A full discussion of dual diagnosis assessment is beyond the scope of this chapter, but to be able to engage in treatment with a client with a substance abuse history, the clinician needs to be able to distinguish whether the presenting symptoms stem from substance use, an independent psychiatric condition, or a combination of both. For example, it is not uncommon for substance users with no separate psychiatric diagnosis to present with those symptoms that are typical of a depressive condition, such as insomnia, irritability, restlessness, anhedonia, lack of motivation, appetite disturbance, and suicidal ideation. At other times, substance abuse symptoms, such as delusions and hallucinations, can appear to be consistent with more serious psychiatric conditions.

On the other hand, those with psychiatric disorders sometimes use substances primarily to self-medicate, and the substance use can mask the seriousness of the underlying disorder. For example, someone experiencing psychosis may use substances that could induce delusions or paranoia, making it seem as if the client's psychotic symptoms are caused by substance use, or someone with significant depressive symptoms could use substances that are activating, thereby masking some of the depressive symptoms. Given that effective treatment approaches for those with primary substance abuse issues differ from treatments for those with primary psychiatric conditions, an accurate diagnosis is crucial to successful treatment.

Approaches to treatment of persons with a dual diagnosis of substance abuse and a psychiatric condition can vary, depending on the treating clinician's theoretical orientation, training, and experience with similar client populations. One approach is to view substance abuse as being of primary concern and psychotherapy as a possible adjunct to meeting the goal of complete abstinence. This approach assumes that mental health problems will most likely resolve when abstinence is reached and sustained. Substance abuse treatment methods range from self-help abstinence-based programs, such as Alcoholics Anonymous or Narcotics Anonymous, to residential or inpatient substance abuse treatment programs. The prevailing format of these substance abuse programs tends to be group treatment because of the many curative factors associated with this form of treatment (Connors et al., 2001). However, the type of behaviors that can lead to successful outcomes in group treatment (e.g., self-disclosure, focus on self, verbal participation) can sometimes be contrary to many traditional Asian values, such as not burdening others with one's problems, keeping one's thoughts and feelings private, and not bringing shame onto one's family by exposing one's weaknesses. Although everyone can benefit from careful preparation before joining a substance abuse treatment program (i.e., via motivational interviewing or other similar preparatory interventions; see Connors, Donovan, & DiClemente, 2001), Asian American clients may need much more preparation to participate fully, and some Asian American clients may not be able to participate in such group treatment modalities at all.

Another approach to treatment of dual diagnosis is to see substance abuse as a symptom of an underlying emotional-psychosocial condition that must be resolved to achieve a long-term positive outcome, which may or may not result in complete abstinence. Although traditional substance abuse treatment views complete abstinence as the primary measure of success, the concept of harm reduction has been gaining more acceptance as an alternative public policy and treatment approach (see websites http://www.harmreduction .org and http://www.harmreductiontherapy.org as examples of such acceptance, and http://www.pubmedcentral.nih.gov to view *Harm Reduction Journal*). The harm reduction approach recognizes that for some individuals, complete abstinence may not be possible or desirable, and managing the associated risks is an acceptable end goal of intervention. Under this approach, gaining insight into one's patterns of behavior and resolving previously unresolved issues and concerns will naturally lead to a decrease in harmful and uncontrolled behaviors, including substance abuse. I take this harm reduction approach in the case discussion that follows.

This case study presents a course of treatment that lasted about 2½ years of an Asian American male with this author. This client's identifying information has been disguised or changed, and when appropriate for illustrative purposes, information from other cases was integrated, which also serves the purpose of further protecting the client's identity. The term *Asian American* is used intentionally in this discussion to protect the client's identity, but the cultural issues discussed here can be applicable to several Asian countries, mostly East Asian countries, such as China, Korea, and Japan. The case presentation is divided into different stages of treatment with the relevant aspects of treatment at each stage discussed.

Vignette: Beginning Stage (First 6 Months)

A is a single, 30-year-old, Asian American male who sought treatment following a DUI incident involving alcohol and cocaine. He was mandated to seek treatment by the court. He had no previous experience with therapy and contacted this therapist based largely on her Asian American ethnicity. A's parents were immigrants to the United States who valued and maintained a rigid hierarchical social structure and customs, and A and his younger siblings were born in the United States. All of A's close friends were of the same ethnic background as his own, and A had a strong sense of "we" versus "they" against the mainstream U.S. culture. Given these facts, understanding A's culture and normative relationship patterns within the culture were crucial to accurately conceptualizing A's case and working with him effectively. During the initial sessions of psychotherapy, time was spent gathering information for clinical and cultural assessment, building rapport and a therapeutic alliance, and preparing him for insight-oriented work.

In terms of substance use, A reported that he started to use cigarettes and alcohol when he was about 16 years old with his friends and began using marijuana and cocaine in college. Although cigarette and alcohol use by men is considered acceptable and to an extent expected within many Asian cultures, illicit drug use is frowned upon because using substances that are prohibited by law suggests a failure of will and is seen as a character flaw and a sign of moral degeneration. Because of these reasons, A hid his illicit drug use from his father and felt a deep sense of shame that prevented him from examining possible reasons for his use. During the few years that preceded the arrest, A used alcohol and cocaine primarily, with occasional marijuana use. A reported that he had stopped using all substances, except tobacco, after his arrest for DUI and that he had been abstinent for about a month at the time of intake. A cited shame regarding the arrest as the primary reason for his abstinence and agreed to continue his abstinence during therapy.

In terms of mental health history, A remembered that he felt angry most of the time starting from his early adolescence. He reportedly always felt he was a disappointment to his father, unlike his siblings, who did better academically and were seen as being more compliant by their father. A reported that he had varying levels of motivation to do well in school, which resulted in a wide fluctuation in grades. Although he was admitted to a university, he dropped out after a year and started to work in a retail job because he did not feel confident that he could succeed in college. This was discouraging for him because he had always struggled to prove to himself and others that he was not "dumb." He expected others to look down on him because he did not have a college degree and was not able to enter a professional field as he was expected to do. He reported that his appetite and sleep patterns have been variable for as long as he could remember, possibly due to his substance use and/or underlying depression, but during recent weeks, he had symptoms of early insomnia (difficulty falling asleep) and significant weight loss due to a loss of appetite. A reported a history of constant anger and irritation that preceded his substance use and a "cloud of sadness." At the time of intake, he reported feeling an acute sense of distress, mostly due to the deep shame of having been arrested and feeling that he failed his father again. He was unable to describe any feelings he was aware of other than feeling angry and "numb." He was often tearful during the initial sessions. In addition to alcohol and cocaine abuse, A was diagnosed with a depressive disorder.

During the first several months of treatment, A's stance in therapy could be described as dependent and guarded. He was guarded in sharing his deep emotions and any information that could be perceived as negative about his family or friends. When he did share some information, for example, that his parents divorced when he was about 6 years old, he denied that he was negatively affected in any way by this event. This was perceived as being culturally normative because one's loyalty lies first and foremost with one's family, both immediate and extended, and then with one's social group, and sharing negative information with an outsider, in this case the therapist, would have been inappropriate.

A also expected the therapist to provide answers to his questions and problems and had difficulty reflecting inwardly about his possible contributions to any problems he was experiencing. In this early phase of therapy, the therapist was viewed merely as a source of information and someone who could hopefully change his behavior, rather than a collaborator in examining and understanding his life and coming to insights that could lead to changes.

Consequently, the first few months of therapy focused on gathering factual information about A's past and current life, providing psychoeducation regarding the psychological meaning of the factual information (e.g., that constant anger, lack of motivation, and a chronic sense of failure could have been signs of depression during adolescence), and finding solutions to immediate problems, such as how to understand and resolve conflicts with coworkers. Any challenges to his culturally appropriate guardedness and dependence at this stage would have jeopardized the therapeutic relationship and may have led to premature termination of therapy sessions.

Efforts were made during this stage to increase the client's awareness of himself by asking reflective questions (such as "What was that like for you?") and making frequent empathic (such as "That must have felt...") and validating statements (such as "I can see how you might feel that way"), with the hope that this would prepare him to participate more fully in insight-oriented psychotherapy. During these sessions, A was constantly angry and regularly reported experiencing interpersonal conflicts with family, friends, coworkers, and even strangers.

Middle Stage (6 Months to About 2 Years)

As therapeutic alliance became stronger and A developed more "emotional language" to express his feelings, A shared with the therapist increasingly more personal and meaningful information regarding his experiences with his family and friends. Contrary to A's initial protestations, one of the most painful events in A's life was his parents' divorce and its effects on his life. As is true in most non-Western cultures, divorce is highly stigmatized in most Asian cultures, and many Asian Americans deal with it by trying to forget. A reported that he and his siblings were never actually told that his parents divorced. He remembered that his mother left one day with suitcases, stating that she was going to visit her family in their country of origin and that she would return "soon." A never saw or heard from his mother again.

In many Asian countries, all children, but especially sons, are viewed as belonging to the father's family, and in cases of divorce, sons are expected to remain with their father. Because divorce is a shameful and stigmatizing experience, maintaining relationships with one's children, and therefore with the ex-spouse, would be a constant reminder of one's failure in marriage; therefore, it is not unusual for one parent to retain full custody and for the other parent to sever all ties, at least until the children become adults. A's father believed and expected, as many Asian parents do, that by removing all reminders of the biological mother and the divorce, the children would eventually "forget" about the now missing mother and adapt to their new life.

We revisited A's experience with his parents' divorce several times during this stage, each time focusing on a different aspect of it. A initially focused on his anger toward his biological mother for abandoning him but eventually arrived at an empathic understanding of her decision to sever ties with him based on cultural expectations. Consequently, he was able to recognize that the divorce and his mother's abandonment of him were not his fault and that she did not abandon him because of his characteristics (e.g., that he was too much trouble) but because she felt she had no other choice.

A bulk of the sessions during this stage focused on A's relationship with his father. Shortly after the treatment began, A's father contacted the therapist to discuss A's treatment. He was informed of the laws regulating confidentiality of privileged information and that the therapist could not discuss with him any information about any client the therapist was working with, without consent to do so from the client. A's father expressed frustration that the therapist would not cooperate with him and his belief that this therapist would not be able to work effectively with A without his help. When the fact of his father's attempt to contact the therapist was shared with A, A decided to avoid any future confrontations with his father by telling him untruthfully that he decided to discontinue therapy. Although this chain of events could be viewed as indicative of dysfunctional family dynamics from the mainstream perspective, they are consistent with A's cultural beliefs. In most Asian cultures, the elders of the family, in this case A's father, assume at least a part of the responsibility for all family members' well-being. In this case, A's father expected to be respected by the therapist in his role as an elder, and when he felt disrespected by the therapist, he assumed that the therapist was incompetent and possibly naïve. Given his position as A's father, it would have been degrading for him to ask his son for permission to speak with the therapist, and therefore he did not pursue that avenue of inclusion into therapy. A's response was also culturally congruent in that he did not wish to include his father in his treatment at that time but felt that he could not go directly against his father's belief[1] that he should be a part of A's treatment.

Even though A lived independently from his father, he visited him frequently, and he still referred to his father's home as "home." In contrast to the seeming closeness between A and his father, there was little discussion regarding personal matters between them, and they argued frequently. A was highly emotionally reactive to his father and became easily agitated when describing their arguments or his feelings about his father. In discussing A's relationship with his father, it became evident that A's reactions to, and expectations from, others in his life were influenced by his experiences with his father. A reported feeling a deep sense of rejection, not only from his mother but also from his father, following his parents' divorce. A reported that his father seemed to withdraw from the children, frequently leaving them with their relatives. There was virtually no conversation between A and his father during these years, except when there were problems and A's father verbally and physically disciplined him. As many children do, A internalized and personalized these events, coming to believe that he was an undesirable problem child, and with no opportunities to examine and correct these beliefs and feelings, he maintained them as an adult. This influenced his relationship patterns with others because he always expected rejection and criticism from them and reacted accordingly. When he gained this insight, A was able to recognize when he engaged in negative relationship patterns and to move beyond his viewpoints and interact with others with more empathy and less combativeness. This change significantly decreased the frequency of interpersonal problems he experienced at work and with his friends.

With A's increased awareness of his feelings and needs and a desire to communicate to his father about his inner experiences, A requested to have joint sessions with his father. This request, if viewed from the mainstream perspective, could be seen as regressive and undesirable, but in this case, it was viewed as an important aspect of treatment for A. Given the cultural expectation that one's relationship with parents is primary, sometimes even competing with one's relationship with a spouse, separation and independence from A's parents was not a culturally relevant goal. It was decided that desirable outcomes from the conjoint meetings would be to decrease the frequency of arguments between them by increasing mutual understanding and to help A "practice" expressing his feelings and needs to his father in a manner that was acceptable to both of them.

During the initial conjoint sessions, some work had to be done by the therapist to gain credibility from A's father. This was important in light of the experience during the beginning phase of treatment when A's father was offended by the therapist and to help A feel confident his father would be comfortable with the therapist. This included reviewing the therapist's academic and professional credentials with A's father, actively demonstrating empathy and culturally sound understanding of the various issues and concerns, using proper terms and titles when addressing A's father, and gently but consistently setting limits, such as not meeting with the father alone and not disclosing information that was previous shared by A in our individual sessions. Over the course of the several months that these conjoint meetings took place, A was able to share with his father how confused and hurt he felt by the events surrounding the divorce and his deep need for approval and love from him. A's father was able to acknowledge and eventually accept A's feelings and to be less critical in his interactions with him. Normalizing many Asian parents' tendency to focus on the things that need to be corrected rather than praising their children[2] helped A's father to not feel blamed and to listen to A's experiences with an open mind.

Gaining insight regarding A's substance use was a constant theme during the individual sessions, especially during this phase of treatment. A decided to resume alcohol use, but in moderation, shortly after treatment began, and one of the treatment goals was to help him manage his alcohol use. As A became more aware of the emotional pain and feeling of loneliness that he endured during his childhood, he came to see that substance use was the only coping mechanism he had available to him during that time and that it was a self-destructive behavior. This insight allowed him to be less ashamed of his drug use and to be able to examine it more openly in therapy. As he came to value himself as a person, internal consequences of drug use, such as numbing of feelings, being unavailable for relationships with others, financial consequences, and feeling out of control with his life, became more pressing and painful than external consequences, such as fearing others' judgment, shame, and legal consequences. This shift allowed him to increase his commitment to abstain from cocaine use, and he found the idea of losing self-control to be unpleasant for the first time in his life.

During this phase of treatment, A relapsed for several months following an experience of rejection from a close friend, and he abused alcohol as well as using cocaine on one occasion. He frequently canceled sessions during this time, and his feelings of loneliness and distress during these months were acute. When he finally felt that the therapist understood the extent of his distress, he was able to discuss his fear of abandonment from this therapist because he felt he failed her by relapsing. He was also able to see the direct relationship between cocaine use and his feelings of rejection and loneliness. This stage of treatment was characterized by A's increased awareness of his feelings, including sadness and loneliness; an increased desire and ability to look to himself to gain insight into problems and conflicts; and an increased desire to engage with others and to form new relationships.

Final Stage (Last 6 Months)

After the successful completion of conjoint sessions with his father and resolution of some of the painful and unresolved issues associated with his parents' divorce, A appeared to be more at peace with himself. Following the relapse, A reported that he recognized the destructiveness of drug addiction and felt no desire to use cocaine again. His relationships with coworkers had improved, and A was making some tentative steps toward making new friends. He no longer argued regularly with his father and felt less of a need to prove himself to others. This stage of treatment focused on consolidating gains, exploring the meaning of the end of our long relationship, identifying supportive resources in his life, and identifying warning signs for relapse. He was invited to return to treatment if he felt he needed to.

Conclusion

This chapter discussed a course of treatment in which an affectively based, insight-oriented approach was applied within the Asian American cultural context. The client's history of substance use was interpreted as a symptom of his underlying psychological and emotional issues, and the treatment proceeded with the assumption that resolving the client's underlying psychodynamic issues would result in a successful outcome in terms of his substance abuse. A caveat should be inserted here that this approach would work only if the client has the ability to abstain from or moderate substance use during most of the treatment and that sustained active use would prevent one from participating in insight-oriented treatment. Sustained active use of substances implies that the client is relying on substances to relieve dynamic tension and, therefore, likely would not be able to bring such tension to therapy sessions to be explored. In such a case, the client should be referred for substance abuse treatment first, before employing an insight-oriented approach. Both approaches can be used simultaneously only if the client appears to be able to benefit from insight-oriented psychotherapy.

It is important in any therapeutic relationship for the therapist to have as accurate an understanding of the client's presenting picture as possible, and it would be impossible to have a reasonably accurate understanding of someone without knowing and understanding their cultural context. Although ethnic matching between client and therapist may not be necessary, available, or desirable,[3] it could help to build empathy and a therapeutic alliance more rapidly. In those cases where the therapist and client are not ethnically matched, it would be crucial for the therapist to become as familiar as possible with relevant cultural factors and to obtain supervision as appropriate.

Notes

1. In this case, the word *belief* is used deliberately, rather than *wish* or *desire*, because A's father most likely did not wish to be a part of A's treatment but probably felt that it was his duty to do so to ensure proper and effective treatment of his son.

2. Humility is a highly prized virtue in many Asian cultures, and it is believed that praising one's children can lead to them to be prideful.

3. Some Asian American clients may prefer not to see a therapist from their own ethnic background because they may feel that it would be more shameful to disclose problems to someone from their own ethnic background than to someone who is further removed from their culture. There may also be concerns about confidentiality and privacy if the community is small.

References

Atkinson, D. R., Maruyama, M., & Matsui, S. (1978). Effects of counselor race and counseling approach on Asian Americans' perception of counselor credibility and utility. *Journal of Counseling Psychology, 25*(1), 76–83.

Atkinson, D. R., & Matushita, Y. J. (1991). Japanese-American acculturation, counseling style, counselor ethnicity, and perceived counselor credibility. *Journal of Counseling Psychology, 38*(4), 473–478.

Atkinson, D. R., Poston, W. C., Furlong, M., & Mercado, P. (1989). Ethnic group preferences for counselor characteristics. *Journal of Counseling Psychology, 36*, 68–72.

Connors, G. J., Donovan, D. M., & DiClemente, C. C. (2001). *Substance abuse treatment and the stages of change: Selecting and planning interventions.* New York, NY: Guilford Press.

Drug use among racial/ethnic minorities, revised (2003). Bethesda, MD: U.S. Department of Health and Human Services, National Institute of Health.

Fugita, S. S., & Crittenden, K. S. (1990). Towards culture- and population-specific norms of self-reported depressive symptomatology. *The International Journal of Social Psychiatry, 36*(2), 83–92.

Greenberg, J. R., & Mitchell, S. A. (1983). *Object relations in psychoanalytic theory.* Cambridge, MA: Harvard University Press.

Kim, L. S., & Chun, C. A. (1993). Ethnic differences in psychiatric diagnoses among Asian-American adolescents. *Journal of Nervous and Mental Disease, 181*, 612–617.

Kim, S. (1998). Differences among Chinese, Japanese, and Korean American students at a university counseling center: Utilization, presenting problems, and effects of counseling variables. *Dissertation Abstracts International: Section B: The Sciences and Engineering, 58*(10-B), 5647.

Kuo, W. H. (1984). Prevalence of depression among Asian-Americans. *Journal of Nervous and Mental Disease. 172*(8):449–457.

Lee, C. L., & Zane, N. W. S. (Eds.). (1998). *Handbook of Asian American psychology.* Thousand Oaks, CA: Sage.

Lee, W. M. L., & Mixon, R. J. (1995). Asian and Caucasian client perceptions of the effectiveness of counseling. *Journal of Multicultural Counseling and Development, 23*, 48–56.

Leong, F. T. L. (1986). Counseling and psychotherapy with Asian-Americans: Review of literature. *Journal of Counseling Psychology, 33*, 196–206.

Lin, J. C. H. (1994). How long do Chinese-Americans stay in psychotherapy? *Journal of Counseling Psychology, 41*(3), 288–291.

Mental health: Culture, race, and ethnicity. A supplement to Mental Health: A report of the surgeon general (2001). Rockville, MD: U.S. Department of Health and Human Services, Public Health Service, Office of the Surgeon General.

Moodley, R., & Palmer, S. (Eds). (2006). *Race, culture and psychotherapy: Critical perspectives in multicultural practice.* New York, NY: Rutledge.

Siegel, A. M. (1996). *Heinz Kohut and the psychology of the self.* New York, NY: Rutledge.

Stolorow, R. D., Atwood, G. E., & Orange, D. M. (2002). *Worlds of experience: Interweaving philosophical and clinical dimensions in psychoanalysis.* New York, NY: Basic Books.

Sue, S. (1977). Community mental health services to minority groups: Some optimism, some pessimism. *American Psychologist, 32,* 616–624.

Uba, L. (1994). *Asian Americans: Personality patterns, identity, and mental health.* New York, NY: Guilford Press.

Wong, E. C., Kim, B. S. K., Zane, N. W. S., Kim, I. J., & Huang, J. S. (2003). Examining culturally based variables associated with ethnicity: Influences on credibility perceptions of empirically supported interventions. *Cultural Diversity and Ethnic Minority Psychology, 9*(1), 88–96.

Index